OPENING THE WINDOW

≈⸰⫷⸰≈

Leaf Seligman

OPENING THE WINDOW

Sabbath Meditations

For Pastor Jack Mzday,
I had the pleasure of attending your
church on 7/31 — your day of celebration.
Clearly you live with the window
wide open so I am standing
downwind to catch the spirit as
it shimmers off of you.
With praise to whom all praise
is due —
love,
Leaf

BAUHAN PUBLISHING
PETERBOROUGH, NEW HAMPSHIRE
2011

Library of Congress Cataloging-in-Publication Data

Seligman, Leaf, 1958-
Opening the window : a collection of sermons / Leaf Seligman.
    p. cm.
Includes bibliographical references and index.
ISBN 978-0-87233-148-8 (pbk. : alk. paper)
    1. Sermons, American--21st century. 2. Unitarian Universalist Association--Sermons. I. Title.
BX9843.S45O64 2011
252.09132--dc23
                                2011026634

Printed in Canada

BAUHAN
PUBLISHING LLC
7 MAIN STREET PETERBOROUGH NEW HAMPSHIRE 03458
603-567-4430
WWW.BAUHANPUBLISHING.COM

This collection is lovingly dedicated to two
of my teachers, both of whom I met in the
summer of 2000 during clinical
pastoral education.

Eckart Horn
1961-2010
priest, mentor, friend, shooting star,
opener of windows

John B. Gustin II
1992-2001
whose wordlessness taught me presence
whose presence brought me grace

Keep knocking.
The joy inside
will eventually open a window
and look out to see who's there.

Rumi

CONTENTS

INTRODUCTION

As a child growing up in the South, the rhythms and vocal textures of various preachers, including Martin Luther King, Jr., floated in the air, creating an aural landscape that summoned me to the window. There, I would peer out, drawn not so much by the words but the feeling: that palpable sense of spirit blowing through.

The process of opening the window has come in fits and starts. I began writing stories in childhood to understand the incomprehensible: within me and beyond. Fiction provided a window into what ultimately felt real. It offered a passageway to the ineffable paved with words: those early stories instructed me in a useful truth: all words are metaphors for what the body experiences. While words matter, they are portals to understanding but not understanding itself. Though they come from deep within, once airborne, printed on the page, even stored in memory, the words we use will dissipate. Ideally what lingers on the sill will be what the words evoke—the presence of spirit flying in and out.

I have been long drawn to the perennial questions: Why do we do what we do? What happens as a result? How do we make sense of, and find meaning in, our lives and in the world that contains us? How do we render wholeness out of brokenness, creating mosaics of beauty and functionality from the rent pieces of our lives?

I have grappled with these questions by writing for most of my life: first through fiction, then plays, and then essays. After many years defining myself as a writer who taught writing in a university and occasionally prisons, I sought a different form and context in order to inhabit the questions instead of just responding to them. The voices that summoned me as a child to the window returned—knocking from inside.

Now, as a Unitarian Universalist minister, raised a Reform Jew, I luxuriate in the joy and challenge of writing Sabbath meditations. More than any other literary form I have encountered, they allow me to weave together story, poetry, reportage, uncertainty, humor, and pathos—drawing on texts made sacred by our traditions and our experience. As an oral art, they rely on cadence and sound, capturing the pulse of life that resonates deep within our bodies and the cultures from which we spring. Though the form arises from particular experience and finite perspective, potentially it can transcend both to encompass more than the sum of its parts. More than any other endeavor, writing and preaching Sabbath meditations invites me to open the window and document grace. *Dayenu.*

Keep Knocking

Truth on My Lips

It is an honor to be invited to preach at an ordination and it is a daunting and humbling task to speak about something as essential as truth-telling, truth-living, and truth-loving, especially in the context of ministry. Had I known just how daunting a task it would prove to be, I might not have said "yes" so fast, but I believe we get what we need, and in the order of service at my ordination I wrote, "God doesn't call the worthy; God makes worthy the called"—thus I am hoping God, in the most expansive sense of the metaphor, makes me worthy of such an awesome task.

When I began to write this sermon I thought: Who am I to tell all these people, many of whom have ministered for far longer than I, anything about the truth? Naturally, I turned to the words of others, writers who so wisely and eloquently speak of truth-telling: Audre Lorde and Adrienne Rich. As I read that early draft aloud, I tried to convince myself that I had written a sermon worthy of such an auspicious and significant occasion. But in my belly I knew something was missing so I emailed the sermon to a very wise and truthful friend of mine—a poet and spiritual director I cherish for her honesty, and she emailed back what my gut already knew: the sermon lacked my presence. In short, it lacked my truth.

And any sermon about truth-telling must tell its own truth. Not someone else's.

I will start at the end and work backwards. What I have to offer this afternoon is an attempt to live my truth, and even to love it, because truth-telling is about telling the truths we are trying to live. All we have to offer as ministers is ourselves. Our full selves—our training, every book we've ever read, the losses we've lived through, the strength of our love, the depth of our anger, the expanse of our limitations, our familiarity with fear, and the stretches of time we find ourselves wandering in the desert, and the lushness of our time in the garden of truth. Ministry as far as I can tell is about being far more than doing. It asks nothing more or less of us than the presence of our full selves. We bring our wholeness, which is to say our brokenness, our healing, our blessing, and our limp.

Many of us know Henri Nouwen's concept of the wounded healer. We know that our suffering informs our capacity to suffer with—to engage in compassion. As apt as the concept is, I find even more compelling the story of Jacob wrestling with the angel, refusing to let go until he is blessed. As they wrestle, the angel strikes Jacob on the hip and knocks it out of joint. Though the angel concedes to Jacob's demand and blesses him, he leaves him with a limp. Rachel Naomi Remen writes that the limp is Jacob's place of remembering. She also writes that

> A blessing is not something that one person gives another. A blessing is a moment of meeting, a certain kind of relationship in which both people involved remember and acknowledge their true nature and worth, and strengthen what is whole in one another. By making a place of wholeness within our relationships, we offer others the opportunity to be whole without shame and become a place of refuge from everything in them and around them that is not genuine. We enable people to remember who they are.[1]

That is the best definition of ministry I know. Simply and profoundly living our truths—telling the truth with our lives and loving the truth in a world where we are taught to fear it—in such a way that encourages others to live and love theirs. As the great cultural critic bell hooks writes, "It is impossible to nurture one's own or another's spiritual growth when the core of one's being and identity is shrouded in secrecy and lies."

---

1 Remen, Naomi. *My Grandfather's Blessings: Stories of Strength, Refuge, and Belonging*, Riverhead Books, 2000, p. 6.

Little more than two years ago, I sat listening to the sermon at my ordination, preached by a man who has taught me more about ministry through ministering to me than anything he could have conveyed in class at divinity school. For all his credentials as a faculty member at Harvard, his ministry to me in a time of profound change and challenge was one of being, of full presence. In his sermon he spoke of my promise as a minister, of my integrity and intellect—indeed I was shiny—and exactly one month after I sat listening to his stirring and complimentary sermon, I withdrew from my first call to a congregation. The details are unimportant and the only reason I mention this is that I can't stand here with any integrity and preach about truth-telling without telling my truth—without saying I wanted to be perfect, or at least stay shiny, bright enough to illumine, as I think many of us wish to. We want to live up to our full potential, fulfill our God- or grace-given talents. We want to earn the respect of our colleagues and mentors and congregants. We want to be loved.

But life on the pedestal is hard—for any of us. It is tiring and lonely and terrifying in a way because we live in fear of falling off, of being found out, of having our rough edges and raw places exposed. But the truth I live is that, like Jacob, I did not want to let the angel go until he blessed me. (Be careful what you ask for.) I got my blessing and it came with a limp—a place of remembering.

We minister from our wholeness, which is to say, in part, our brokenness. I needed to break some more because like the Leonard Cohen song says, "Ring the bells that still can ring. Forget your perfect offering. There is a crack in everything. That's how the light gets in."

I overturned the pedestal and cracked open in ways more painful and profound than I could have imagined—ways that allowed the light to touch those secret places of shame. And I found out what we all need to know in order to minister, that Julian of Norwich is right: "If there be anywhere on earth a lover of God who is always kept safe from falling, I know nothing of it—

for it was not shown to me. But this was shown—that in falling and rising up again we are always kept in the same precious love."

In our falling and rising up again our feet of clay, like Jacob's limp, become a reminder of our blessing. There is no greater blessing than to have your life's work lie in those moments of meeting—that certain kind of relationship, one-to-one and within a congregation where each one remembers, like Jacob, and acknowledges one's own and the other's true nature and worth. When we as ministers acknowledge our own true nature and worth, only then can we bear witness to and affirm the true nature and worth of others.

The year I withdrew from that call I volunteered as a chaplain in a county jail. Every week I would sit with men and women whose lives had been disrupted—broken apart—by addiction, poor choices, a lack of resources, faulty systems, a lack of compassion, a shortness of truth. I sat with folks who felt powerless, whose lives were upended, their futures uncertain. People who had not fully faced their anger and damage and grief. I would sit and listen, nodding because I identified, and without having to tell them what was happening in my life as I teetered on the brink of my recently chosen vocation, I lived my truth with my presence and my compassion. I knew in my belly I was supposed to be there, searching for the light in each person I met and reflecting it back.

I share this story because it was that volunteer chaplaincy—a year of afternoons sitting in a county jail—that allowed me to pick up the pieces and grout them into a tabletop, not a pedestal, of function and beauty—to realize that our truths include our brokenness, our imperfections. The broken pieces in each of us may be sharp and scary but when we set them in the grout of that "same precious love," in the grout of accepting our wholeness, our mistakes and vulnerabilities, and the fact that some of our truths will frighten others because "we are taught to fear the truth, to believe it always hurts" (bell hooks) then we can experience and minister from the blessing that accompanies the limp.

As ministers, we are called not only to live our truths but to love them. And love, which so often gets sentimentalized, romanticized, and trivialized, is no easy endeavor. To love the truths of ourselves and others means we must be willing to recognize the evolutionary nature of truth. Like rivers, truths flow and bend, merge and meander; occasionally they dry up but most often they course steady as blood, enlivening us. To love truth in a society that thrives on lies—political and personal deceits, lies about appearance and affection, loyalty and satisfaction—is to be countercultural in a radical way.

M. Scott Peck says "Love is an act of will—namely, both an intention and an action. . . . We do not have to love. We choose to love." So we can choose to love the truth just as we can choose to practice generosity. We can choose to answer honestly when someone asks "How are you?" or "Do you think I'd be a good person for that committee?" We can choose to love our truth when someone generalizes or maligns a culture or sensibility to which we belong or that belongs in us.

We can choose to love our truth as ministers by letting our displeasure show, by acknowledging the limits of our responsibility, the limits of our patience, the limits of our experience and expertise. We can choose to love the truth by being authentic.

I remember losing my cool in a meeting and later apologizing to the board and committee chairs after the others left the room. The board chair said, "It's probably good they saw you get upset. It's good for us to realize you have your limits."

The truth isn't always pretty but it is beautiful, because truth expressed responsibly and respectfully is always a liberating force. The truth frees us to be and to bring our wholeness into each moment, to experience blessing as

> a moment of meeting, a certain kind of relationship in which [the] people involved remember and acknowledge

their true nature and worth, and strengthen what is whole in one another. By making a place of wholeness within our relationships, we offer others the opportunity to be whole without shame and become a place of refuge from everything in them and around them that is not genuine.[2]

Ministry is a way of being that, when done truthfully, allows and encourages all of us to remember who we are: in our fullness, our brokenness, our beauty and our truth.

May it always be so.

2 Ibid.

The Virtue of Disappointment

Two big religious holidays are right around the corner: Passover and Easter. While there are historical linkages between the two—Jesus is thought to have arrived in Jerusalem to celebrate Passover the day before the Romans crucified him—there is another connection as well. In the Passover story, God summons Moses to go to Pharaoh and demand that he release the enslaved Hebrew people. Moses isn't so keen on the plan initially, but he goes, and as instructed, after much wrangling and many plagues, he leads the Israelites out of bondage. But liberation is not all it's cracked up to be. "The whole congregation of Israelites complained against Moses and Aaron in the wilderness. The Israelites said to them, 'If only we had died by the hand of the LORD in the land of Egypt, when we sat by the fleshpots and ate our fill of bread; for you have brought us into this wilderness to kill this whole assembly with hunger' " (Ex16: 3).

In short, the Israelites, having endured slavery for their whole lives, finally make it out only to find their leader has brought them to a wilderness and a hunger they have never known. Imagine if you will the profundity of disappointment. Consider real live people who have spent their lives indentured. Imagine the time your life felt most constricted by circumstances you believed were out of your control. Recall your weariness, your longing to be free of constraint. Finally, after an imperiled escape, you and your family are now in the hands of a leader you have never before met, a man who tells you God Almighty called him to the task, a man who insists you trust in the LORD, who, by the way, may have ushered you out of slavery, but hasn't packed a lunch for you as you leave.

Imagine how crestfallen you might feel realizing you have risked everything to get out of Egypt, but at least in Egypt there was food. Can you conceive of the disappointment? In God? In Moses? In life itself? When we are in touch with our own disappointment it is easier to imagine someone else's.

So imagine being Moses, or his brother Aaron, conscripted by God into unprecedented service. You have managed, not by your own wit, to get thousands of Israelites out of danger, and now they grumble out of a hunger you yourself cannot relieve. In that moment before God rains down manna, imagine the disappointment Moses might feel in God for making him the stooge to his people. Or perhaps Moses experiences disappointment in the people who doubt God. Such ingrates, he might think, to complain about hunger after being freed from generations of bondage.

Once the manna falls from heaven, it continues for forty years, but imagine wandering even on a full stomach for forty years. If you recall the time in your own life when it felt most bleak, can you remember envisioning relief? Better circumstances? Perhaps someone suggested things would improve in time. But forty years later, you have no clue where you are, where you are headed, what will happen. And by now, you are getting thirsty.

"The people quarreled with Moses, and said, 'Give us water to drink.' Moses said, 'Why do you quarrel with me? Why do you test the LORD?' But the people thirsted there for water; and the people complained against Moses and said, 'Why did you bring us out of Egypt to kill us and our children and our livestock with thirst?'" After forty years wandering in the wilderness, the Israelites are disappointed still. Into their disappointment, God brings water from a rock. But still, they have not reached Mount Sinai, and at last when they do, Moses goes up the mountain. Again the people wait. They have been walking their whole lives. The youth of the young has been spent, the aged are frail, the once fertile now barren. For forty days the people wait for Moses to come down. Sure, they want news of this Almighty God who has brought them out of slavery and, only when nudged, given them food and finally water, but still no sign of the Promised Land.

The people get tired of waiting. We may think, What's forty days more after waiting forty years? but the people have had enough. Their patience has worn from thin to nothing, so they gather around Aaron and ask him to make gods for them. Aaron instructs them to take off their gold jewelry and with it he fashions a golden calf. The people make offerings and "The LORD [says] to Moses, 'Go down at once. Your people, whom you brought up out of the land of Egypt, have acted perversely; they have been quick to turn aside from the way that I commanded them.'"

Notice when the Israelites disappoint God, they suddenly become Moses', people, not God's chosen ones. It's the same tone we use when a child or parent or pet disappoints us and we say, "Can you believe *your* fill-in-the-blank did that?" We are quick to deny connection when disappointment erupts.

In the end, God simmers down, controls his anger, and renews the covenant he has made, but not before he makes his wrathful disappointment clear.

Yahweh of the Hebrew Scriptures has been disappointed by humans before. Adam and Eve, Cain, all the creatures who didn't get a spot on the ark. It seems in fact that the creatures God supposedly creates in God's own image end up disappointing God on a regular basis. Who would create progeny destined to disappoint?

Every parent who ever lived.

That's the kicker. Disappointing each other is inevitable because we have expectations. We have an experience we wish to re-experience but then it turns out differently. Everything doesn't go according to our plan. Or we have an experience we long to leave behind that revisits us, in one form or another. In many ways the Exodus narrative is a family drama writ large.

In every family, parents hope for their infant a good life, a better life. Most parents attempt to instill decency and desired values. They want their kids to make smart choices, often smarter choices than they made back when they disappointed their own parents.

And just as surely, parents disappoint children. Spouses disappoint one another. We needn't trot out the names of politicians recently dragged through the mud this past year: the tales of infidelity and indiscretion that not only humiliated but disappointed very visible wives, to say nothing of voters.

I recall the deep disappointment I felt in my father when he was not able to provide for his children; that he moved far away and lost touch when I needed him most. I recall the disappointment I felt that he never established a relationship with my sister. He just didn't know how. In turn, I have disappointed many people and I know I will disappoint more just by being human.

If we are wrought in the image of God, or some kind of planetary goodness or cosmic genius, because truly, human life is a wonder to behold, then we are shaped by a creative force that breathes disappointment into our lungs as surely as air.

Consider the story of Jesus at Gethsemane. He has celebrated the Passover Seder and foretold his own betrayal. He goes to the garden agitated and grieved, and asks his disciples "to remain here and stay awake with me." Jesus, clearly distraught, throws himself on the ground and prays. When he stops, Jesus sees the disciples have fallen asleep. "So you could not stay awake with me one hour?" he asks. Twice more the disciples disappoint him by not remaining awake, by not keeping him company in his time of anguish.

In the Christian tradition, Jesus is divine, so here again we have a representation of God experiencing bitter disappointment. And for those who relate to Jesus as human, imagine your own vigil before death. Imagine the ones you are closest to falling asleep as you implore them to remain awake with you.

Think of the ways we all manage to fall asleep, metaphorically. The ways we lapse in our full presence and attention. We blink at another's suffering to avoid feeling the fullness of their pain, or perhaps our own as it gets mirrored in someone else's. It isn't easy and perhaps it isn't possible to remain awake, to stay present every time someone needs us to. Our own hurt, our exhaustion, our fear, our self-contempt can bring on sleep. Can make us blink, tune out, or turn away.

This season that brings both Passover and Easter poignantly reminds us of the importance of staying present in the presence of disappointment. What's instructive to me in these ancient narratives is not their historicity, but their truth. It is inevitable that we will experience disappointment: not just our own but the disappointment our action or inaction causes. Sure, it would be great if we could all dispense with any hint of expectation or desired outcome, but few if any can. So we are left with our own humanness. Our own narratives contain many threads where our needs get tangled in another's expectations or vice versa.

I can still see the disappointment written across a previous congregant's face when I expressed a feeling that collided with hers. She burst into tears. I had not intended to upset her nor did I think I had uttered something terrible. I tried to speak my truth with love. But she had her own version of truth, her own expectations of me, and however unrealistic I found them, she felt them. I am clay-footed like everyone else. We both had to find a way to live with and move past the disappointment. That's the tricky part, at least for me. One has to be able to acknowledge it *and* let it go. To hold on to it like some flattened penny in the bottom of the sock drawer, pulled out on occasion and rubbed like a talisman of regret, does no good. But nor does it work to ignore disappointment, to pretend the wince that flashes across a face is something else.

Congregations, like families, don't often speak openly of the disappointment that peppers our interactions, but there is value in doing so. Acknowledging disappointment invites us to be accountable and it demonstrates our limits—the boundaries of what we can tolerate and accommodate. And it teaches us when and where we snap.

It is good to make room for disappointment, to speak lovingly in its midst, mindful that we walk in all the light we have. It's useful to identify the inner source of our disappointment as well as what we perceive as the external cause, remembering that disappointment arises when our expectation or desire goes unmet. It doesn't happen *to* us so much as it wells within us.

By the end of the book of Exodus, God has renewed the covenant with the Israelites. The Scriptures don't give voice to the disappointment of tribes and nations God destroys, but we can infer. They do however reveal that disappointment—divine and human—never truly wanes. But neither does solace, which arises from connection. We need each other and thus we are compelled to reconnect. And when we can hold each other in our disappointment, we bless each other by acknowledging our true nature and worth. Too often, the shame of disappointing a person we love or respect compels us to turn away, deny or justify too quickly what we've done. But if we don't give up on each other, and instead commit to hearing each other out, we reap the benefit and offer the blessing of inhabiting our full selves.

God liberates the Israelites so that they will enter into a covenant of responsibility. And according to the story, the Hebrew people still have to wander for forty years. They hunger and thirst, fear and despair, and ultimately are delivered, but there are no guarantees what they are delivered unto.

Jesus suffers disappointment as cruel as his crucifixion yet he teaches his followers that it is better to let go of past hurts. Better to rise from the ashes and brush oneself off. Neither betrayal nor disappointment—a son's anguished cry to his father, a mother's heartbreaking inability to save her son—must have the last word.

May we endeavor instead to stay awake, to remain present—and *when*, not *if*, we falter, may we hold ourselves and one another accountable in loving embrace. In the mirror of our disappointment may we glimpse our humanity and a glimmer of the divine.

Reclaiming Sin

Sin. It's a word most religious liberals, especially Unitarian Universalists, avoid, so why do I seek to reclaim it? Why in my bathroom do I have a "purified plastic wash-away-your-sins shower curtain for liars, cheaters, and wrongdoers"? Why the shower scrub that lets me "make amends as I cleanse"? Because the two friends who've known me longest insisted I buy it out in Seattle. "How fitting," they both said, each offering to buy me accompanying hand cleanser and body wash. I had to agree, as I was preparing to move into my new apartment in a building renovated from an old Baptist church. Fitting indeed. But several years before the shower curtain and living in a converted church, something else nudged me.

Back in the spring of 1998, I attended a reunion at my private grammar school. Sitting in the parking lot with the woman who had been my best friend from second until seventh grade, we faced the windshield, letting our sentences rest unseen in the cavernous dark of her Chevy Suburban. In the past twenty-five years we had spoken twice, snippets, not conversations, nothing of substance. All those years, I wondered why she had so abruptly dismissed me, announcing one day when we were twelve that she no longer wished to be friends. Finally alone with her in the car, safely ensconced in adulthood, I confessed my curiosity about her sudden rejection so long ago. She surprised me by revealing the bitter hurts of her childhood, which truthfully I had not considered. Then, our conversation turned to God. She sent her children to a Christian academy. At that time, I talked to trees. I spoke not of God but of the benevolent universe. She asked, *What do you do with your sin?*

Resist calling it that, I thought. So much of sin boils down to fear. Fear of not belonging. Fear of being judged. Self-centeredness.

She turned and faced me. *You're not so different. We all have pain.*

If that same woman from my childhood were to pose her question today, I would tell her not only do I want to reclaim sin, I want to discuss it with the congregation, even if it scares people. Admittedly, until this woman from my childhood asked me about my sin, I didn't think about it either. In my Reform Jewish family, we did not talk about sin, though we discussed many things sinful: racism, greed, exploitation, injustice. Sin got relegated to what felt like outmoded religious ideas from somebody else's closet. Sin had to do with shame, carnality, lust. Or guilt, which we discussed enough. Sin fueled the rhetoric of radio evangelists far more than it entered the discourse of my parents, who sought to teach me about the evils of injustice without ever characterizing injustice as sinful. Failing to make that connection constitutes a lost, but not irretrievable, opportunity.

As a religious liberal, I want to recast sin as not living right-sized, and see it as an invitation to *recognize* our own grasping, which might allow us to *re-evaluate* how we live—the resources we use, our mindfulness relative to other beings, and the relationships we form. The potential arises to meaningfully atone for the sin of self-centeredness by attempting right relation.

Living right-sized implies balance, and it relies on humility and an awareness of others. We can't be right-sized if we notice only ourselves. Many of us experience deep connection at the water's edge, gazing at the stars, or in the woods, standing silent and still enough to observe birds or deer. In those moments, we understand the importance of being right-sized. If we are too loud or too visible, or gobble too many natural resources, we will lose the trees and shorelines that soothe us, the animals that stir us. But so often, we leave those quiet beautiful places, get in the car, and turn on the radio. News of the world floods in, in ghastly torrents. Newscasters report such global and persistent horrors that, were he here, Noah would ready the ark.

How to live right-sized in the paradox of postmodern life,

where I read *Bon Appétit*, with its glossy spreads of "ethnic" foods available in specialty markets online, knowing full well that most of the denizens in countries of "exotic" cuisines barely subsist on gruel or rice. When I lived in Maine and used to delight daily at the sight of deer in my back yard, their presence signaled an uglier truth: the vast expanse of woods and pasture turned into subdivisions and shopping malls. Great scabs of blacktop accommodate bigger and bigger vehicles trying to squeeze in to get those bargains made by small hands in faraway lands.

The sin of not living right-sized is not about being born with an inescapable stain. As religious liberals, we do not subscribe to a doctrine of so-called "original sin." We have inherent worth, not inherent sin. The sinfulness, however, arises out of our very humanness: our desire to belong, to feel secure, to leave a mark. It arises in the grasping that fuels overconsumption.

I am here and can go anywhere, the SUV roars. *I belong to this milieu*, the designer label declares. *I'm worth listening to*, the advanced degree asserts. *I am deserving of a little comfort*, the latest gadget announces. All of us connected in our grasping, in our heart-felt longing, in our search for meaning. When we notice what we want and others need, what others want and we need, we see that living right-sized is not as simple as giving up resources, though sharing them more equitably would help. Living right-sized means living in right relation to all being. And that's no easy task. That's a lifetime of spiritual practice with no graduation or recital at the end. Living right-sized is a calling we wake to each day.

Sallie McFague, in her book *The Body of God*, writes, "sin is our refusal to stay in our proper place." By figuratively and literally grounding sin in the existence of planetary beings who must share physical space, McFague offers a model of sin comparable to not living right-sized. She urges us to locate our proper place and proportion relative to our species and all others. Just living demands that humans, as self-aware creatures, recognize and respect competing needs for space.

McFague's ecological theology carries political and economic implications with it. To hoard resources, to mine and strip and fell, to breed other species for slaughter, gambling, or to conduct tests upon them, to send satellites into space to gather information or improve cable reception, are human acts that plump us into "haves" while simultaneously increasing our appetites. Because these actions affect the universe as a whole and foster imbalance, they cannot be viewed in isolation as simple odes to human ingenuity; they also demonstrate what McFague identifies as "plain old-fashioned selfishness—wanting to have everything for ourselves."

Hubris, better known as the deadly sin of pride, factors into the sin of not living right-sized. Process theologian Gordon Kaufman notes sinfulness within the hubris of thinking we know it all. He writes,

> . . . whenever we try to overcome, and thus control the ultimate mystery . . . through . . . confident affirmation of theological or philosophical ideas we think we *know* are true . . . we are actually attempting to make *ourselves* the ultimate disposers of our lives and destiny; and thus we sin. . . .

There's much in liberal religious tradition that historians and theologians have pointed to that engenders resistance to naming the sin of wrong size. Perfectionism, rationalism, humanism, the Enlightenment, modernity, individualism, the great frontier and expansionism—all invite us to justify our grandiose sense of self and size. But until we name the sin of not living right-sized, we will not redress it. Our failure to do so restricts us as much as those who live in our shadow. The point is not to pander to guilt, which is ultimately self-serving, but rather to heed what Unitarian Universalist ethicist Sharon Welch proposes: a love of self and other as the driving force behind an accountability that shifts the focus away from self-centered guilt to a community-centered responsibility.

While those of us who enjoy privilege and access to resources reacquaint ourselves with humility, those without privilege and access must avert diminishment. Our tasks differ depending on our social location, but we each share in the process of transformation. Whereas many people of privilege deny any culpability for the imbalance of resources, others who claim responsibility must guard against reducing people with fewer resources and less power to a singular status of victimhood. To assume that only those who have more can shift the balance, without the participation of those who have less, perpetuates the sin of not being right-sized. We inadvertently slip back into the hubris and omnipotence we need to avoid.

In order for each of us, regardless of social location, to determine our right size, we need to explore the lines of connection, both buried and visible. For those of us who sit squarely in the realm of plenty, we must invite the perspective of those who do not occupy the same realm. We need to endure the fear of being viewed critically by those we have alienated or exiled to lives of unjust deprivation.

Frequently, we experience the temptation to define the terms and the solutions, rushing in to fix something by controlling the process instead of listening first. When we try to salvage or save without honoring the agency of those in need, we spare ourselves from acknowledging how our actions may contribute to, or cause, problematic conditions. Setting ourselves up as the savior fosters the illusion that only heroic or superhuman acts make us worthy.

I understand this impulse. I spent years unwittingly drawn to people I thought I could heal, with the dexterity of Jesus, in a desperate attempt to heal myself. I inhabited that paradox of self-centered insecurity that made me feel responsible for the world's suffering and its repair. So it is with compassion that I recognize the temptation to swoop in and mend seemingly irreparable tears.

But what happens when one group claims to know what's best

for another? And how difficult is it to acknowledge self-interest while appearing altruistic? Living right-sized demands an answer. Obviously, circumstances exist when one group, as in the case of an elder who prevents a one-year-old from toddling into an open well or fire, knows better. On the other hand, many a worker in the movement to assist battered women has had to learn that telling a disempowered adult what she needs to do inadvertently disempowers her further. Living right-sized means respecting the agency of each person, especially when a person's choices don't align with our own.

For many Unitarian Universalists and other religious liberals whose values and upbringing reflect the post–World War II surge of productivity and technological advancement, agency becomes activity that expresses vitality. We equate stillness with inactivity and impotence. Industry and mobility protect us. Consumption imparts security. The more we have, the bigger we feel. So we keep moving, keep doing, keep acquiring, exercising our options, which may entail out-sizing and overpowering others. Then to justify that, we may turn to theologies or ideologies to support our behavior. Without meaning to, we trade our Unitarian Universalist values of respecting the interdependent web of existence and fostering justice, equity, and compassion, for intellectual dominance and the global export of goods, dissatisfaction, and ideas.

As humans, we seek to belong, to feel secure in our place, to leave our mark yet sometimes, perhaps inevitably, we miss the mark. That is one of the connotations in Hebrew for the word *sin*. We expend such energy making a mark; we would do well to examine the ways we miss it. We seem to be the only species that builds monuments to ourselves. If we recognize our presence within and relationship to all being, could that be the affirmation of purpose and belonging we hunger for?

To speak of sin is not to talk of hellfire and damnation, of repression and carnality, but of hubris and the need to live right-sized. If we ignore "the inescapable network of mutuality, tied in a single garment of destiny" that Martin Luther King, Jr. so aptly named, we will miss not only the mark but the possibility to transform the moments when we fail to do so. Reclaiming sin is an invitation to live right-sized, and what could be better than that?

Why Universalism Still Matters

During my ministry in Ontario, I got a call the week before Christmas from a woman who wanted to know if the congregation was Universalist. She explained that she had been raised in a fundamentalist Baptist home in the American Midwest, and only Universalism offered her the possibility of life without the fear of eternal damnation in Hell. Since she identified herself as a Trinitarian, not a Unitarian, I referred her to a liberal Christian church I knew of, but long after the call ended, her question haunted me because it brought into clear relief the fact that lots of people really do worry that they will end up in Hell, as evidenced by the recent cover story in *Time* magazine by Jon Meacham entitled "What If There's No Hell?" Meacham brought to light the controversy surrounding a new book by the popular young pastor Rob Bell, whose Universalism may be old news to us, but to many traditional Christians, it's fiery hot.

Universalism was a theological response to the Calvinistic doctrine of predestination, where only the few elect souls, predetermined before birth, would be saved and the rest would end up in Hell, It shook eighteenth-century Christianity to its foundations. Though Universalism as a theology and a denomination did not formally emerge until the late eighteenth century, the Greek philosopher Origen articulated a version of it around 225 CE. Not surprisingly, he was martyred in 253, fifteen hundred years before John Murray brought the concept of Universalism to the United States in 1770 when his boat ran aground of the New Jersey shore.

By the 1920s, most mainline Protestant denominations accepted some version of universal salvation that meant that Universalism as a denomination lost its edge, though clearly among fundamentalists it remains hotly debated.

For the woman who called me in Ontario, Hell is no laughing matter. During that ministry I volunteered as an on-call hospital chaplain and I recall being summoned to the critical care unit to pray with a family gathered around a man expected to die shortly, as life support and heroic measures were about to be discontinued. When I asked the man's wife if there was anything special she wished me to lift up in prayer, she replied, "Yes, can you pray he'll be forgiven?" She told me he was a good man, except for the alcohol. I looked into the eyes of his grown children gathered there. For them it appeared his goodness had been obscured. Alcoholism has a way of doing that. Again she asked me, "Do you think he'll be forgiven?" "Yes," I replied, "I certainly do."

The experience underscores the spiritual reality of many still pained by the possibility of being doomed to an eternity of alienation and isolation. For a lot of people, this is a terrifying thought, and it serves no one, least of all us, to dismiss such fear as ignorant or superstitious.

For most of us, Hell it is a condition we encounter here on earth—arising from greed or a lack of compassion, and an unwillingness to honor the connections that bind us. It manifests in the gross disparity between haves and have-nots, in the objectification of beings: human, animal, and botanical objectified and commodified as resources. Hell manifests when our resentments enflame into rage. But there's another way Hell on earth becomes a condition of our own making, and it arises when we ourselves become alienated from our religious roots.

Our legacy as Unitarian Universalists means that we not only respect the inherent worth and dignity of all, but we respect the power of such an affirmation, that we take the time to let it sink in and fully understand the profundity of what it means to say that every person has inherent dignity and worth. That no human being must earn it. We have it by virtue of our being. And as beings with inherent dignity and worth, we will not be consigned to suffer endlessly in any phase of life, be it the one we now inhabit or some past or future phase we cannot behold. But here's where our Universalism gets tricky, and demands much of us: If Hell on earth is comprised of avoidable suffering perpetrated by humans, then what does it mean for us to participate, collude, or even benefit from—through our decisions, our consumption, our economic and political systems— the suffering of others?

If we believe that all people have inherent dignity and worth, that all people, and hopefully all beings, will thus remain part of the collective experience we know as life; if we believe that all people are bearers of light and capable of goodness, what is the implication when we diminish the potential in others, when we obscure their light or use up the energy sources they need to experience illumination? What happens to us when we violate our own decency by exploiting others or reaping the benefits of exploitation?

We mean well. We are good-hearted folk. We respond to disasters, but what happens when we overlook the ongoing crises?

Universalism compels us to look at the world head-on and not blink. It asks: Can we hold in our minds and hearts the possibility that each person will occupy the same place at the metaphorical welcome table? Perhaps it is easier for religious liberals to dispense with the idea of Heaven or Hell than to have to consider spending eternity with the likes of anyone who perpetrates terror and violence around the globe.

We may think we have the luxury to dispense with Heaven and Hell as theological constructs, but for the hellish conditions we allow, or contribute to, however unintentionally, how will we answer? Suddenly, it is not others with their quaint desire to be forgiven, to be freed from the fear of eternal damnation: it is we who must reckon with our own forgivability. It is we who must face the challenge of walking our talk, of knowing we walk in all the light we have and thus, extending that understanding to others, while holding them and ourselves responsible for our actions.

For religious liberals, and humanists in particular, there may be no external source that threatens us with damnation: only our own psyches that register disappointment when we fall short of our potential, when we fail to fulfill our capacity for compassion, courage, conviction. Those of us who have sought forgiveness and still believe *we* have inherent worth may find it easier to believe others are worthy of another chance.

Redemption lies at the heart of Universalism—the possibility that our next action can somehow redeem the last one, or the lack of one. Universalism is a doctrine of possibility, of promise: not just a promise of reconciliation with the divine, but reconciliation with ourselves and our fellows.

In an age where all our technological and scientific advances have not eradicated the hellishness of war, the pervasiveness of hunger and preventable disease, the inequity of resource distribution, we would do well to remember and embrace Universalism. Spreading its gospel allows us to welcome others while acknowledging the spiritual realities we all face, not just those we consign to religious conservatives.

Two centuries ago, people feared Universalism because they thought without the threat of Hell people would not behave. Universalists countered that it was the assurance of God's love that would inspire people to behave. Who wants to disappoint a loving and benevolent creative source?

Today, humanism compels many of us to reach our full potential as human beings endowed with reason, critical thought, creativity, and morality. To squander our uniquely human gifts would be disrespectful to ourselves and whatever evolutionary processes have brought us to this point. Yet for all our potential and the many ways we each fulfill it, we still fall short as a species. The suffering we create and permit does not speak well of us. Our postmodern Universalism calls us to task. It underscores our connection with all being—demanding that we not blink, that we remain accountable to each other, that we consider what it means for all beings to gather at a welcome table where some of us pushed and shoved to ensure a chair.

Universalism still matters because it is only in an uncondemned state that any of us can change. Because the essence of who we are here and now is at stake. And those of us who belong to a denomination named for it are no less in need of its promise of redemption than anyone else.

Of Shoes and the Sacred

Like a lot of women and, I suspect, some men, I love shoes. I'm a Doc Marten aficionada. For those of you unfamiliar with Docs, as they are affectionately called, they started out as boots for the British workingman and they mysteriously took off in popularity with young hipster Americans in the early 1990s. I traveled to Brighton, England, to buy my first pair. I went in search of the only authorized "vegetarian" Docs, made of synthetic leather right there in Brighton. It was during my "I don't buy leather shoes" phase. As it turned out, the boots rubbed horrible blisters and I gave them away. Many years later, I bought my second pair, clunky black wingtips you've seen me wear, also manufactured in England. By the time I bought my third pair of Docs, brown oxfords, I noticed they were made in Thailand, as were my latest acquisition, the purple ones.

Sadly, Doc Martens have gone the way of Nike and Converse and Keens, all made elsewhere. We can only hope the shoes we wear are not manufactured in sweatshop conditions. Footwear used to be a proud American-made product, but with few exceptions only the hype is produced here. If it seems too late to reclaim the industry, take heart from the recent example of the Girl Scouts of the USA who put their uniform manufacturing out to bid. While Girls Scouts USA had a clause requiring vendors to adhere to "strict guidelines about worker age, treatment, and safety," news of the bidding process evoked an onslaught of requests from parents, members, and volunteers to keep the manufacture of uniforms in the U.S., and the organization did. Perhaps public pressure could bring the manufacture of shoes home.

We spend twenty-five billion dollars a year on shoes in the U.S. Though probably not representative of this congregation,

Glamour magazine reports the average woman in the United States will buy 469 pairs of shoes in her lifetime. Even those of us who lack the Imelda Marcos penchant for shoes—if we add up all the shoes we've ever had, including the ones that get shoved to the back of the closet, bought on a whim or gone horribly out of style, or just too darn uncomfortable to wear, we accumulate scores of shoes over the years. Even men who stick to black and brown, dress and casual, and maybe a pair of athletic shoes can gather a collection. Anyone who's ever bought shoes for children knows how fast they outgrow them.

Shoes don't just cover our feet. They function as props in the play of our lives. The first pair of dress shoes—where we first wore them. The moment of passion when we slip off our shoes. The imprint of flip-flops or sandals on a favorite beach.

Our preference for and memory of certain shoes dates us: provides a timestamp, geography, and social location. Do saddle shoes, wingtips, Weejuns, Sperry Topsiders, Keds, or Buster Browns ring a bell? What about those clunky old hiking boots with bright red laces? Or are you conversant with Diesel and Sketchers, Yellow Box and Chinese Laundry? Steel-toed Wolverines, Herman Survivors? Dependable old loafers or colorful Crocs?

Shoes are artifact.

Urban legend is full of shoes. Young men have been shot over a pair of Air Jordans. From basketball courts to *Sex in the City*, from soccer cleats to state-of-the-art running shoes, from a pricy pair of Manolo mules to Florsheims polished to a mirror shine, shoes carry stories, not just our feet.

What are your shoe tales? Do you remember the first pair you bought? If you have children, do you remember theirs? My mother kept my brother's baby shoes in a beautiful antique curio cabinet with a glass door. All his little white shoes displayed on green velvet. I spent hours as a pre-schooler playing shoe store, lining up my stuffed animals, fitting them with my brother's outgrown shoes. When my brother and I were small, there were not all the precious little baby and toddler shoes available now.

But I do remember a pair of cherry red oxfords and a matching pair in navy blue, buttery soft Italian leather, wildly extravagant for a six-year-old. Purchased by my mother on a trip to New York. My early childhood favorites were my first pair of high-top sneakers, a reward for being brave at the dentist when I was four. And at six, I picked out my first pair of white bucks. Just like Dr. Kildare. Another reward for bravery at the dentist. Shoes narrate the string of cavities I had as a child.

They attest to miles traveled, destinations reached. When people die, there's a poignancy to shoes left empty, the way they hold the scent and shape of feet, an intimate portrait left behind.

Shoes become metaphors as we speak of "big shoes to fill." We remind one another not to judge a person before walking a mile in his or her shoes. At Franklin Pierce University, there's an annual event to raise awareness about domestic violence called "A Walk in Her Shoes," where men are encouraged to literally walk in women's shoes to experience how it feels.

But for all the money we spend and the metaphors we use, a billion people worldwide go without shoes, a third of them children. How do you walk a mile in the shoes of someone who has none?

During the second Sudanese civil war, when thousands of the Lost Boys (and a number of girls) walked hundreds of miles to escape, most walked barefoot. Every day, people in places rife with infection, parasites, and inadequate or nonexistent sanitation go shoeless because they can't afford them. None of the thirty thousand shoe stores in the U.S., not even Zappos or Endless.com, can reach the folks living in makeshift tents and lean-tos of discarded tin, relegated to refugee camps or roadsides, or stuck between active railway tracks. In Latin America, Africa, Asia, children wander barefoot. Teenagers travel in shoes four sizes too small. Adults do their best to scuff along in fragments of shoes so worn they barely hold together. In Romania, Mongolia, and the Ukraine, where it's cold half the year, people need boots and sturdy shoes. When many refugees from the Southern Hemisphere arrive in North America they often wear sandals year-round. Right here in the United States, when hurricanes, floods, and wildfires devastate areas, thousands of people need footwear.

As a child who relished shoes, it did not occur to me to imagine living without them, though when I think back to the kids who lived maybe a mile or two away on a dirt road aptly named Hardscuffle, their dark brown feet were usually bare. For them, hookworm was probably a reality, along with calluses and cuts and endless dust.

It was a single shoe washed up on the beach after the tsunami hit Indonesia in 2004 that compelled a successful shoe company executive named Wayne Elsey to rally his associates in the industry to collect 250,000 pairs of shoes. After Hurricane Katrina, he did it again, and then realized he needed to keep going. He started the nonprofit organization Soles4Souls with the simple goal of providing shoes to people in need. Right now, they give away a pair of shoes every seven seconds. But Wayne wants to make it a pair every second until the need for new shoes becomes obsolete.

When I first read about the possibility of traveling with Soles4Souls to help fit shoes, I flashed back to myself at three, slipping the paws of teddy bears and stuffed kittens into my brother's white booties and orthopedic saddle shoes. I can do this, I thought. I do not know how to build houses or pour concrete foundations or lay bricks, but I can fit shoes. I can wash feet; in fact, I have wanted to participate in that religious ritual since I first heard of it in seminary. Before Jesus was reputed to have washed the feet of his disciples, washing the feet of one's guests was a sign of hospitality in the Ancient Near East.[3] In the book of Exodus, "the washing of feet is required of those who are to come before God at the Sanctuary."

_____

3 *Anchor Bible Dictionary*, vol. 2, p. 828

Most religions have rituals around purity or ablutions, but the spiritual cleanliness of washing feet can be as much a way to sanctify the washer as the washee.

From the thirteenth chapter of the Book of John:

> During supper Jesus . . . got up from the table, took off his outer robe, and tied a towel around himself. Then he poured water into a basin and began to wash the disciples' feet and to wipe them with the towel that was tied around him. Jesus came to Simon Peter, who said to him, "Lord, are you going to wash my feet?" Jesus answered, "You do not know now what I am doing, but later you will understand." Peter said to him, "You will never wash my feet." Jesus answered, "Unless I wash you, you have no share with me." . . . After he had washed their feet, had put on his robe, and had returned to the table, he said to them, "Do you know what I have done to you? . . . I have set an example that you also should do as I have done to you."

It is an example I want to follow. The humility and intimacy sanctifies both parties. If shoes *tell* a story, feet *illustrate* it with their pungency and naked truth.

Our feet connect us to the earth, to what is real and sacred, which is why God instructs Moses to remove his sandals so that he can feel the ground, holy beneath his feet.

Holiness isn't something ephemeral or amorphous that exists out there in the ether or the firmament. Holiness is what occurs in the moment of alchemy when any of us chooses to be fully present to another.

Joan Chittister, the great Benedictine nun, writer, and activist I often quote from, recounts a personal story of her daily commute in her book *Welcome to the Wisdom of the World*:

> I began to notice, there was one solitary man standing back off the roadside at the edge of a ragged corn field, a flag in his hand, a sign by his side, one small camp chair open and

planted behind him. Trip after trip. Week after week. In cold rain and sleet, in hot sun and wind, there he stood, alone and totally silent. Keeping watch, eloquently silent.

One day, I simply turned the car around and went back, drove down the berm slowly, and stopped. . . . he wore army fatigues, and, on the broomstick standard that he held in one hand while he waved with the other, he flew a homemade flag with a peace sign on it. "Give peace a chance," the sandwich board sign propped up by the chair read. He himself, I realized as I got closer, had braces on his legs.

He was just one man with one small peace sign standing on an empty road waving a homemade flagpole back and forth at every car that passed.

In my mind, that single man, a veteran I presume, goes on waving every day of my life. It was his persistence, his dogged refusal to give up waving, his single-minded commitment to changing my mind that got me. . . .

When all is said and done, "persistence" is the antidote to powerlessness. When I refuse to go on waving, when I pick myself up and leave the field, I have given in. I have surrendered my soul to forces whose only argument is that doing what is wrong is better than doing something else. But it is not the glory of the Chinese government and its use of repression to maintain order that the world remembers —and applauds—after the rout at Tiananmen Square. It is the sight of one young man standing in front of a tank. . . .
In the end, the sight of goodness undeterred has more power than all the forces on earth arrayed against it.

For every pair of shoes we give to someone who needs them more, we sanctify the labor of those who cut the pattern, sewed the shoes, filled the box—often working in a sweatshop. We sanctify the sacrifice of animals whose skin becomes leather. We sanctify the persistence of a million Haitians still living in tents. We sanctify the persistence of the lost boys and girls who walked for years out of oblivion and sometimes back into it. We sanctify the persistence of immigrants who reach our shores yearning for a better life, wearing sandals in St. Paul or Chicago or Boston because that's what they have and they will not let what's on their feet stop them from moving.

We, the abundantly shod, who collect our surplus and send it to those in need: let us remember, on the eve of Valentine's Day, that while the health, lo, the survival, of millions hangs in the balance, *our* humanity dangles there, too.

In the book of Isaiah, the prophet writes: "How beautiful upon the mountains are the feet of the messenger who announces peace, who brings good news, (52-7).

Let our feet be made beautiful not by our shoes, but our willingness to shed them—that we might feel the ground holy beneath us, made that way not by some distant god, but by the earth itself and the immanence of people who dare to persist.

Lessons From Haiti

Let me begin by saying this is not the sermon I wrote coming home on the plane. That attempt remains un-transcribed from my chicken-scratch penned in a pocket-sized Moleskine notebook. All week I struggled with what to share and wondered why I felt no impulse to write. I went to Haiti expecting to be transformed. I went to wash feet, to be humbled by that moving ritual of intimacy, and in so doing, to serve. I went to bear witness to a ravaged nation, to a people who persist in the face of extreme deprivation. I went expecting to come back less at peace with my abundantly comfortable life. And though I rinsed many feet—of women and men, children and babies, and bore witness to the ruins wrought by an earthquake and a far more complex set of problems, I return with the understanding that I may have helped but I did not serve.

In her book *My Grandfather's Blessings: Stories of Strength, Refuge and Belonging*, doctor and teacher Rachel Naomi Remen writes:

> Unlike helping and fixing and rescuing, service is mutual. . . . True service is not a relationship between an expert and a problem; it is far more genuine than that. It is a relationship between people who bring the full resources of their combined humanity to the table and share them generously. . . . Service is a relationship between equals. . . . Over forty-seven years of illness I have been helped and fixed by a great number of people. I am grateful to them all. But all that helping and fixing left me wounded in some important and fundamental ways. Only service heals.

I wish in no way to diminish the value of help in the form of a pair of shoes that arrives unbidden. I agree with Remen's assertion, "When we bless others we offer them refuge from an indifferent world," and while mission trips *intend* to offer refuge from indifference, the catch is in the word "blessing," which Remen defines "not [as] something one person gives another [but] a moment of meeting, a certain kind of relationship in which both people involved remember and acknowledge their true worth."

The truth is, without humanitarian aid many people would starve, die even sooner, and suffer more. But the other concomitant truth is that relentless aid creates a relationship of dependence that keeps us from coming together in our shared humanity, because after a while, the donor becomes a dollar sign and the recipient a manifestation of need. Then it is not one's true nature and worth being recognized, but rather a predetermined role. Whether we want it to or not, charity always maintains imbalance.

For the most part, the blessing I experienced in Haiti happened with my wonderful tripmates and our local liaison John, a soulful man who moved to Haiti twenty-two years ago. We spent all day and evening together sharing our stories, our experience, our faith, our questions. We played cards and laughed, ate meals together. John offered his vast knowledge of Haiti and our group leader Katie afforded us ease of travel. Both provided a rich opportunity to experience a glimmer of Haiti viewed from several facets. I found value in every moment of the trip and returned so grateful but, in all honesty, my encounters with Haitians could not constitute blessing because the interactions lacked "that certain kind of relationship" Remen writes of where "*both people involved* remember and *acknowledge* their true nature and worth."

The people who sat across from me with a basin of water between us understood they were there to receive shoes, not share their gifts. The shoes no doubt will be helpful and as much as I want to believe those folks felt my presence and desire to rinse their feet as a gift, the fact that they had no opportunity to offer theirs, and had no role other than recipient, kept the moment from blessing us. I suspect some, perhaps a few, would have preferred to rinse their feet unassisted. Having me pat their feet dry as a mother might do for her children may have been an indignity quietly endured instead of the tenderness I meant to give. Because of the language barrier I could not ask their preference.

The year I volunteered as a jail chaplain, during a time of tremendous upheaval in my life, I knew every time I got buzzed through the massive electronically controlled door that I wasn't there to help; I was there to serve. Every visit, I brought with me my unspoken brokenness. I have told the story many times of a day I arrived feeling fragile, grateful for the distraction of another's woe. I sat with a man I met with every week named Darrick who was a fervent Christian. As usual I asked if he wanted to pray. He caught me off guard by responding, "Yes, Leaf, I'd like to pray for you." That he recognized my humanity by acknowledging my true nature and worth was the prayer. The words he offered up to God were proverbial icing on the cake. What made that encounter a blessing is that Darrick saw me in my full humanity, as a pastor and person with sorrow of my own, and in return, I gave him the gift of pastoring to me.

Allowing someone to meet us in the valley of need is a gift when shared. The gracious patient Haitians who accepted free shoes allowed me with my good intentions and big heart to express my desire to "offer refuge from an indifferent world." But in a world punctuated with charity the imbalance of every sentence suggests a grammar of indifference.

Remen writes, "Service is free of debt." It is devoid of obligation or imbalance. In Haiti the children we visited at an orphanage, and the women with babies, and the students and teachers at an elementary school who received shoes didn't get to bring anything other than their need.

Our religious impulse, lo, our very humanity, calls us not just to do all the good we can, but to do better, and with the least harm. Fostering dependence causes harm. That's why the Zambian economist Dambisa Moyo entitled her first book *Dead Aid*.

So as we give away shoes, how might we invite local folks who receive them to share their gifts with us? The resourcefulness, patience, persistence, and abiding faith evident in Haiti makes it clear the Haitian people have much to share: be it through singing together, or teaching well-meaning missionaries to cook, paint, sew, carve figurines, or make jewelry as they do. At the orphanage we visited, a girl about seven named Vanessa asked not that I take her picture as so many of the children did; she asked that I let her take pictures herself. She made a series of self-portraits and happily went about photographing images arresting to her eye, to her sensibility, not mine. That was a moment of blessing when she escaped the role of an orphaned, deprived child with legs so bowed she could barely walk and I escaped the role of benevolent white do-gooder with a pocket full of toys to bestow like Santa— and the two of us became photographers together.

What I learned in four days is that Haitian people don't want to beg or rely on endless aid. They hustle every day just to exist; they sell used shoes or clothes or quart jars of gas, components harvested from used electronics, colorful pills in blister packs and a host of products that come from somewhere else. The once fertile fields lie fallow, woodlands have been cut, factories sit empty. Charity and missionaries pour in offering compassion and relief, but Haitians like any people seek self-determination. As nice as it is that the shoe company Teva gives away shoes I paid over a hundred dollars for, wouldn't it be even better for the folks receiving the give-away shoes to choose them?

I love the Tevas I bought last summer, but I chose them after looking in no less than a half dozen stores. I passed up several other models of sensible waterproof hiking shoes in search of the perfect pair for walking my dog in the woods. I couldn't help but think as the women at our first distribution slipped off their simple black lightweight loafers or flip-flop style sandals, would sporting a pair of thick-soled leather lace-ups perfect for mountain trails suit their urban tropical life?

We've all heard the phrase "Beggars can't be choosers," but

these were not beggars; they were women who waited patiently for hours because they could use another pair of shoes. When we get shoes we select them. As adults we pay for them, which affords us dignity because we get to exchange something we have for something we need.

What if we were to multiply the good we do donating dollars and gently worn shoes by participating in a longer-range vision as well, so that there can be an end to charity and a regeneration of Haitian agriculture and manufacturing? What if, in addition to the microbusiness Soles4Souls promotes by helping folks in Haiti (and elsewhere) sell used shoes as street vendors or even shopkeepers, it partnered with investors to recapitalize local manufacturing? Why not work toward Haitians producing the shoes, new or used, other Haitians sell?

One of the women on the trip is a shoe designer who wants to go back to Haiti in April. She told our group leader she feels she has so much more to give. And as loving and light-filled as she was, shaking hands with the women whose feet she washed, what if she were eventually able to teach a score of Haitian women how to design shoes? What if the CEO of Soles4Souls shared his vast entrepreneurial and management skills with future Haitian shoe company executives instead of just asking American ones to donate shoes?

What if the droves of good-hearted missionaries arriving daily in Port-au-Prince were to preach a gospel of agency and self-determination?

As Unitarian Universalists, we respect the interdependent web of life and a free and responsible search for truth and meaning, which is to say we understand the limits of self-reliance and value the importance of participation and co-creation. We all rely on a host of beings and elements other than ourselves. In some ways the very notion of an individualized self is illusory. We share DNA not just with chimps but mice and breathe the same air. We survive not by dint of our own grit and innovation, but by the heat and light of a distant star and a watery mineral-rich earth we mine to keep the forges burning and cell phones ringing. We endure because our forebears resisted giving up, and because the bees continue to pollinate and the rivers still run. We overpopulate the planet not simply from our procreational zeal, but because we haven't yet managed to deforest all the trees.

There is a vast difference between inter-reliance and dependence, hubris and humility, self-sufficiency and charity.

Each week in our worship we recite, as part of our covenant, "Love is the doctrine of this church, the search for truth its sacrament and service its prayer."

Service, as Rachel Naomi Remen suggests, "is a relationship between people who bring the full resources of their combined humanity to the table and share them generously . . . a relationship between equals." A relationship between a chaplain and inmate where both get to offer a prayer. A relationship between a young Haitian girl who longs to shine her light capturing it through a lens and a middle-aged privileged American who longs to be of use. A relationship between a graceful surgeon who came to Haiti as a young man to help build a church and school, still there two decades later, and the baby in the orphanage who naps peacefully on the man's chest as he stretches out on the floor of the nursery also in need of a nap.

"Service," Remen writes, "connects us to one another and to life itself. When we experience our connectedness, serving others becomes the natural and joyful thing to do." As we know from compassion fatigue, "fixing and helping are draining"—not just to the helper, but the help-ee. Always being the recipient is tiring, while service—which is mutual—renews and sustains.

As soon as I registered to go on the shoe distribution trip, I expected the experience would be utterly transforming, though I had no idea how. Each day in Haiti, be it sitting with a toddler in my lap or driving by shanties of deprivation, I kept waiting for the transformation. As I conversed with the four generous, soulful women who traveled there with me, as I listened to John recount how he learned to perform surgery prior to medical school from an eminent surgeon who nurtured his skill because he saw a country in need, I felt blessed to be in such fine company. Each day, riding along cavernously rutted roads, whether visiting an orphanage, distributing shoes, or walking amid the rubble of a cathedral destroyed in a city of tents, I witnessed patience, persistence, and faith as never before. The transformation I went in search of was not what I could have imagined: that truthfully, much as I wanted to serve, I had helped. There is value in helping, virtue in giving, but *service is the prayer.*

Food Democracy

From the first chapter of Genesis:

> God said, "See, I have given you every plant yielding seed that is upon the face of all the earth, and every tree with seed in its fruit; you shall have them for food. And to every beast of the earth, and to every bird of the air, and to everything that creeps on the earth, everything that has the breath of life, I have given every green plant for food." And it was so. (vs. 29-30, NRSV)

That is food democracy. The radical yet at one time commonplace idea that all beings "have the right to an adequate, safe, nutritious, sustainable, food supply."[4]

A lot has happened since the sixth century BCE when those verses were likely penned. The great farmer-poet-essayist Wendell Berry writes,

> By farming we enact our fundamental connection with energy and matter, light and darkness. In the cycles of farming, which carry the elemental energy again and again through the seasons and the bodies of living things, we recognize the only infinitude within reach of the imagination. . . . We align ourselves with the universal law that brought the cycles into being and that will survive them.[5]

Food is about relationship: ours *with* the earth, the elements, the soil, the animals, the plants, and each other. Food expresses our relationship to justice and moral sensibility. Because food springs from and relies on death as much as it assures life, there is a primacy to our relationship with food like nothing else. Thus

---

4 http://fooddemocracy.wordpress.com/

5 Wendell Berry, "The Use of Energy," *The Unsettling of America*

our relationship with food, not just what we eat, but how we eat and by what means, forms a core of our spiritual and physical being.

The word "religion" comes from *religare*. To refasten, to return to what binds us as beings to one another, and to whatever we find holy. How we relate with food and its creation or production either refastens us to what matters—what is sacred in us and around us—or it sets into motion a deep sense of alienation—from each other, the earth, the elements, the plants and animals, the soil and cycles, life itself.

Right now in the world, here and abroad, we have loosened the ties that bind dangerously far. By replacing the agrarian with the industrial to the point where small farms are under threat of extinction and local economies have been largely usurped by a global one, it's not simply that people no longer have access to an adequate, healthy, sustainable food supply; nor is it simply that we have traded our souls for sugary non-nutritive edibles that no longer resemble food. We have traded farming for factories, and exchanged the energy of work for dependence on fossil fuels and chemical fertilizers. We have cut billions off from food supplies and self-reliance. Two weeks ago I preached on wandering in the wilderness. The state of our relationship with food has turned the garden of Creation into a barrenness more bitter than wandering itself.

Again, Wendell Berry:

> The word *agriculture*, after all, does not mean "agriscience" much less "agribusiness." It means "cultivation of land." And *cultivation* is at the root of the sense both of *culture* and *cult*. The ideas of tillage and worship are thus joined in *culture*. And these words all come from an Indo-European root meaning both "to revolve" and "to dwell." To live, to survive on the earth, to care for the soil, and to worship, are all bound at the root of the idea of a cycle. It is only by understanding the cultural complexity and largeness of

the concept of agriculture that we can see the threatening diminishments implied by the term "agribusiness."[6]

John Peterson, a third generation farmer and the subject of a documentary called "The Real Dirt on Farmer John" puts it this way:

> You've got two types of agriculture.... One is the agribusiness model, or the chemical model, and it's very, very dominated by capital. The other model is powered by something that may not be inexhaustible, but it's more inexhaustible than capital. It's powered by what I call a moral principle. You have people who are inspired by a moral impulse in relating to the soil and relating to the food, to the farmers and to the planet.... There was no community supported agriculture farm in this country 20 years ago. Now there are maybe as many as a million people being fed from about 3,000 CSA farms—from zero to a million. This came out of human beings just deciding how to spend their money. It's an incredible thing.[7]

On an international scale, "agriculture remains part of the global capital market. Peasant, indigenous, and family farmers cannot compete with the rules of free trade, which are biased toward multinational corporations. Small producers suffer not only from failed domestic policies but also from the consequences of economic globalization."[8]

If we take a look at the seven principles affirmed by the member congregations of the Unitarian Universalist Association in relation to food and the means by which we get it, a path out of the wilderness emerges.

---

6 Ibid.

7 www.bioneers.org/campaigns/food-farming-1/articles-interviews/the-real-dirt

8 www.otherworldsarepossible.org/food-sovereignty

Let's begin with the seventh principle and work backward. Our seventh principle affirms our respect for the interdependent web of all existence. If we are to embody the respect we espouse for the interdependent web, how we nourish ourselves is the literal expression of embodiment.

Dr. Vandana Shiva, who founded the Research Foundation for Science, Technology and Ecology, writes,

> Our study on "Biodiversity based organic farming: A new paradigm for Food Security and Food Safety" has established that small biodiverse organic farms produce more food and provide higher incomes to farmers. [They] contribute both to mitigation of and adaptation to climate change ...especially in Third World countries [where they] are totally fossil fuel free. Energy for farming operations comes from animal energy. Soil fertility is built by feeding soil organisms by recycling organic matter. This reduces greenhouse gas emissions. Biodiverse systems are also more resilient to droughts and floods because they have higher water holding capacity. ... [9]

In the U.S. we "consume 17% of our fossil fuel . . . to grow . . . food with fossil fuel fertilizers, and use diesel on the farm, and use diesel to move the food and process [it]"; [10] we subsidize industrial farms that grow corn, soy, and cotton while insisting that poorer countries lower tariffs. Yet our seventh principle is about decreasing toxicity in the soil, water, air, plant, animal, and human life. It's about stopping the assault on nature, which is to say the web of existence that contains us all.

Our fifth and sixth principles call for the right of conscience and the democratic process, with a goal of world community with peace, liberty, and justice for all. This means food sovereignty:

9 "Biodiverse Ecological Farming is the Answer, not Genetic Engineering" Dr. Vandana Shiva

10 www.bioneers.org/campaigns/food-farming-1/articles-interviews/beyond-the-barcode-the-local-food-revolution

"The right and freedom to grow diverse and nutritious food and the right to have access to save healthy adequate and affordable food" (Vandana Shiva). As Haitian farmer Jonas Deronzil says, "People in the U.S. need to help us produce, not give us food and seeds. They're ruining our chance to support ourselves." All over the world, people strive to regain food sovereignty, from Haitian farmers vowing to burn Monsanto's hybrid rice seeds to farmers in Thailand and South Korea "educating their people about the effects of global trade policies and pressuring their governments to respect the role of farmers."[11]

In the U.S. we call it food democracy, not sovereignty, but it's the same thing: "food with the farmer's face on it."[12]

Our third and fourth principles call for acceptance of one another, encouragement of spiritual growth, and a free and responsible search for truth and meaning. This entails examining our food practices and beliefs, not just individually, but as a congregation. What we eat and serve in community. We're off to a good start with fairly traded coffee and chocolate, and milk from small local dairy farms. And think of the impact we could have buying the land on Fisher Road and gardening it—not just for ourselves, but some of Fitchburg's more recent immigrants who may have farmed in their home countries but now live in a city without land of their own to grow—or enough money to buy—healthy fresh food.

When we talk about our future, let us remember that our principles call us to spiritually evolve, to search responsibly, not to sit satisfied. When we have an opportunity to restore our relationship with food, to nurture in our children and in the wider community an appreciation for the earth and its cycles and our embedded connection, let's not hold back.

Our first and second principles affirm the inherent worth and

---

11 www.otherworldsarepossible.org/food-sovereignty

12 Ibid.

dignity of all and express our commitment to justice, equity, and compassion. There's no way to do that if we turn from the reality of food insecurity worldwide. A billion people lack access to clean water or adequate and healthy food. Concentrated Animal Feeding Operations, or CAFOs, yield cheap meat by denying the dignity or worth of animals and desecrating the environment.

Marion Nestle, professor and former chair of the Department of Nutrition, Food Studies, and Public Health at New York University, says: "I see nationally everywhere people who are increasingly concerned about the quality of what they're feeding themselves and their children. This is grassroots democracy in action."

It matters what eggs we buy. It matters to the chickens, the land, our children, and ourselves. When we resist advertising that markets unhealthy products in packaging that gobbles resources instead of insuring people have enough nutritious food to eat, we live out our principles. When we realize the complexity of decisions like buying Stonyfield organic yogurt, thinking it's a New England company that buys from local farms, only to learn the blueberries are trucked in from eastern Canada and strawberries flown in from China, we wrestle with what a responsible search for truth really means.

We cannot solve a global problem ourselves but we can make local choices that impact the world. At the heart of food democracy or sovereignty is a local economy. In the words of Michael Pollan, "Local food economies are our best hope for checking the drift toward the total global economy. And food is where these economies begin."

Wendell Berry writes,

> People are trying to find ways to shorten the distance between producers and consumers, to make the connections between the two more direct, and to make this local economic activity benefit the local community. . . . This is the only way

presently available to make the total economy less total. . . .
To be a consumer in the total economy, one must agree to
be totally ignorant, totally passive, and totally dependent
on distant supplies and self-interested suppliers.[13]

In the Spring 2011 *UU World* magazine, Susan Bagby, a member
of a New Mexico congregation, writes of her family's efforts to
buy locally. They purchase a share in a CSA farm, only to be so
inundated with eggplants they decide not to re-enroll the next
year; but they continue to buy most of their produce from a local
farmers' market.

In the same issue, there are letters to the editor about
Monsanto's ethics, or lack thereof, and an article by Rev. Kate
Braestrup about the value of beginning a meal with a table grace.
As she says, "Saying grace can remind us every meal is holy."
Across our denomination, we are re-evaluating our relationship
with food.

To be sure, it is a relationship fraught with geo-political and
environmental complexities, but as a starting place we can give
thanks whenever we eat and participate in food production to
the extent we can. We can garden and prepare meals together;
we can learn the origins of the food we buy and the ingredients
in them. Whenever possible we can buy locally grown or raised
food. We can educate ourselves as a congregation about food
democracy and food tyranny, and from that stance of knowledge,
act and activate for change. We can listen to farmers and insist
that our elected representatives do, too. We can find out why the
farm bill in Congress is a food bill that affects us all. We can learn
best practices for farming and gardening and come to each meal
with a deeper awareness of what goes into it, how it gets to us, and

---

13 "The Idea of a Local Economy," reprinted in *The Art of the Commonplace:
The Agrarian Essays of Wendell Berry*, edited by Norman Wirzba

whether or not it refastens us, or moves us further apart.[14]

What binds us as beings is the need for food. How we are bound together—in a relationship of mutual respect or exploitation, mindfulness or ignorance, sustainability or profit—is up to us with every bite we take.

God said, "See, I have given you every plant yielding seed that is upon the face of all the earth, and every tree with seed in its fruit; you shall have them for food. And to every beast of the earth, and to every bird of the air, and to everything that creeps on the earth, everything that has the breath of life, I have given every green plant for food." And it was so (vs.29-30, NRSV).

To paraphrase Wendell Berry, Let us not make shoddy the work of God.

---

14 The bulk of these ideas come from Wendell Berry's essay, "The Pleasures of Eating," published in the book *What Are People For?*

A Meditation on Memorial Day

Tomorrow the bells will toll for fallen soldiers—men and women who have nobly sacrificed. Cities and towns will have parades. Members of the American Legion and VFW posts will place flags on graves of servicemen and -women. Politicians will make speeches. Veterans will offer remembrances of fallen comrades. At Arlington National Cemetery taps will be played, wreaths will be laid, and the Tomb of the Unknown Soldier guarded in solemn ritual. And all the while war will rage on.

The fallen soldiers, airmen and -women, sailors, marines, guardsmen and -women barely whisper from their graves. Quieter still are the fallen civilians.

There is little more sobering than poring over the faces of war dead. Inch-square portraits, row upon row filling pages of the *Washington Post*, the *Globe* or the *Times*. Such earnest visages rendered in miniature as if their lives, their call to service, and their wrenching deaths could be contained in an image the size of a thumbprint. While the photos momentarily arrest us, like a lock of hair falling forward we brush from our eyes, the battalions of images have yet to indelibly inscribe the futility of war.

Of course there have always been pacifists among us. One of my favorites within our tradition is John Haynes Holmes, born in 1879 in Philadelphia and raised Unitarian. John Haynes Holmes helped found the Unitarian Fellowship for Social Justice and what became the American Civil Liberties Union. But for most Unitarians of his day, Holmes's absolute pacifism went too far, and he disassociated himself from Unitarianism during World War I. In 1925, John Haynes Holmes authored his tenth book, *Patriotism Is Not Enough*, published by my grandfather. In it Haynes wrote, "The result of all this sacrificial heroism was—what? Death, destruction, despair—the bankruptcy of nations, and the wrecking of civilization. . . . . Little was won; well-nigh everything, material, ethical, spiritual was lost."

It's fair to say Holmes, like the other absolute pacifists among us, fall out of favor with the majority, who may dislike war, but nonetheless believe in its inevitability if not its efficacy. Of course the profiteers of war, the military industrial complex identified by President Eisenhower, may not dislike it, but most of us on a gut level understand the profits war generates come at tremendous social cost.

Yet beyond the circle of Gold Star families and veterans who know first hand the "death, destruction and despair," beyond the hundreds of millions of non-combatants worldwide who have suffered the physical, political, economic and environmental devastations of war, the rest of us may register such ravages intellectually, yet we assent with our silent acceptance, our complacency and complicity.

I am not suggesting we like war or approve of it, even though we may have the utmost appreciation and respect for the valor of fighting forces. Some may harbor frustration that killing even in the name of national defense gets valorized because killing on foreign soil or sand begs the question: What risk to our life or limb are we defending? And what spiritual and ethical principles do we sacrifice in the process of increasingly roboticized warfare where the faceless enemy becomes even more abstract?

We all know the stories of a Christmas ceasefire where young troops in Europe paused in their trenches, smoking cigarettes, singing "Silent Night" together across enemy lines in English and German. Probably far less chance wary young Americans in Iraq or Afghanistan will pause to set down arms and sing Qu'ranic verses with local combatants, whether they long for safety and self-determination, too. Surely no songs fill the air beneath predator drones.

As staggering as war is for combatants, it victimizes women and children beyond compare. The rapacious hunger for oil, minerals, and other resources has turned their torsos into battlefields.

In her eloquent and moving keynote address to the 2010 Women's Nobel Initiative International Gender Justice Dialogue, social psychologist, writer, and Benedictine sister Joan Chittister said at the turn of the last century, civilian casualties were 5 percent of the war dead. In World War I, 15%. World War II, 65 percent. By the mid 1990s, 75 percent. Today, civilian deaths comprise over 90 percent of war deaths. "If you want to be safe," she suggests not as sardonically as it sounds, "join the military."[15] Major-General Patrick Cammaert, former commander of UN peacekeeping forces in the eastern Congo, concurs when he states, "It has probably become more dangerous to be a woman than a soldier in armed conflict."

I will spare you the grim list Joan Chittister provides but in summary, she calls the sixty million civilian deaths in the twentieth century "an orgy of war and civilian slaughter."

It is not that the deaths of our military should go unnoticed, unheralded, it is that for each tiny portrait published in the newspaper, another dozen faces or more belong in those pages. For while we may distinguish between the patriotism or economic need of men and women who enlist, who join officer training programs or the National Guard—over and against those who simply die in the line of fire—the breath of life that animates each of us, the cosmos that bears us, the creative wellspring that brings us into being weeps no less for the lone boy ambling across the road, the elderly couple hiding in their home, or the hundreds of thousands of women and girls broken by systematic rape meant to brutalize them and shatter their communities with the blunt force of shame.

It is not simply that war happens, Joan Chittister tells us, it is that entire societies are organized around war. "Our generation,

---

15 Dr. Joan Chittister, closing keynote address, Nobel Women's Initiative, 21 April 2010

yours and mine, has made the whole world into prey but only some are armed." Where, she asks, in the monuments we erect to the war dead, are the monuments to those whose lives have been denied not just from stray bullets and bombs, from predator drones and landmines, but from soil erosion, deforestation, diversion of water and food and natural resources used to fuel combat? Consider the children who go uneducated, the women who remain illiterate, the houses that go unfinished, the roads that go unmade, the minds and hearts and bodies untended because there is war—not in our yard but in our name. And not just ours, for there are many nations with denizens so depleted it takes nothing to grind them into fodder. Yet so often the line of connection eludes us. We don't see how our consumerism intersects with war.

Sixty Minutes recently reported on "conflict minerals" in the Democratic Republic of Congo. According to the broadcast, there are over a million displaced people, over teo hundred thousand women raped, and five million deaths in eastern Congo from a civil war "being fueled by a multi-million dollar trade in minerals that go into our electronic products."[16]

Cell phones, computers, even jewelry bears the bloodstains and misery of a nation despoiled. *Sixty Minutes* interviewed a woman in a refugee camp who told of her village destroyed in 2007, where 280 people including her parents and husband were burned alive. Later three of her children were shot dead and she suffered rape by uniformed men armed with machine guns. Her story, horrifically, is common in Eastern Congo, where there are no monuments to war dead, only mineral exports that supply our demand for instant access and communication.

It will not be parades or statues, wreaths or speeches that absolve us or honor the dead. In the words of Joan Chittister, "It's not what the mind knows; it's what the heart knows that changes the world."

---

16 www.enoughproject.org/conflict-minerals

In 2009, a Democratic representative from Washington State, Jim McDermott, introduced legislation to "put in place a system of audits and regulations that would help stop companies from importing conflict minerals into the United States," though the bill has not gained passage. As important as that piece of legislation may be, what lies before us is the willingness to re-see war from the heart, not the mind.

It is excruciating to see in the cell phone we use to call home in an emergency, in the laptop I use to write this sermon, the inconceivable costs of war, from the pillaged earth and polluted air to rape and child labor, burning flesh to immolated villages, to displaced millions in despair. It is hard enough to watch *The Hurt Locker* and imagine negotiating a landscape pocked with IEDs.

But as Joan Chittister and John Haynes Holmes dare to assert, war is not the inevitable consequence of evolution. It comes from a willingness, in some cases couched as patriotic fervor, and sometimes in complicit assent. If it is "only with the heart that one can see rightly," if "what is essential is invisible to the eye" (Antoine de Saint Exupery), we will have to look beyond the convenience to its costs. We will have to listen more closely to what the soul knows and the mind denies. Too often we have conflated entitlement with God's grace, ingenuity with providence, war with religion.

Joan Chittister says, "Violence defines religion consumed more by the national than the universal." John Haynes Holmes sharpens the image:

> Patriotism has its holy days, its saints and martyrs, its sacred books and documents. In its national anthems it has hymnology, in its ceremonials of the flag, a ritual as august as the mass. . . . And it is this religion of patriotism which denies and defeats the ideal of brotherhood, the love of all mankind.[17]

---

17 John Haynes Holmes, *Patriotism Is Not Enough*, Greenberg Publishers, 1925

In 1986, an international group of scientists in fields ranging from neurophysiology to behavioral genetics, ethology to psychology addressed the question of whether scientific theories and data can legitimately justify the claim that war is hard-wired into us. These scholars concluded it is not. In a statement on violence adopted by UNESCO, they arrived at five propositions:

1. It is scientifically incorrect to say that we have inherited a tendency to make war from our animal ancestors....War is biologically possible, but it is not inevitable, as evidenced by its variation in occurrence and nature over time and space.

2. It is scientifically incorrect to say that war or any other violent behavior is genetically programmed into our human nature.

3. It is scientifically incorrect to say that in the course of human evolution there has been a selection for aggressive behavior more than for other kinds of behavior....Violence is neither in our evolutionary legacy nor in our genes.

4. It is scientifically incorrect to say that humans have a "violent brain." While we do have the neural apparatus to act violently, it is not automatically activated by internal or external stimuli.

5. It is scientifically incorrect to say that war is caused by "instinct" or any single motivation.

The signatories of this research statement conclude

. . . biology does not condemn humanity to war, and that humanity can be freed from the bondage of biological pessimism and empowered with confidence to undertake the transformative tasks needed. . . . Although these tasks are mainly institutional and collective, they also rest upon the consciousness of individual participants for whom pessimism and optimism are crucial factors. Just as "wars begin in the minds of men," peace also begins in our minds. The same species who invented war is capable of inventing peace. The responsibility lies with each of us.[18]

This Memorial Day we can do something far more meaningful, far more consequential than marching or attending a parade, more lasting than placing a wreath, flag, or flower on a grave. We can begin the task of changing our own consciousness, of undoing a lifetime of cultural imprinting that has stamped the inevitability of war on our brains. Joan Chittister reminds us: "War is not inevitable. It is chosen; it is planned."

The great Kentucky poet and farmer Wendell Berry asks:

> Who has invented our enmity? Who has prescribed us hatred of each other? Who has armed us against each other
> with the death of the world? Who has appointed me such anger that I should desire the burning of your house or the destruction of your children?

> Who has imagined that I would destroy myself in order to destroy you,
> or that I could improve myself by destroying you?

> Who has imagined that I would not speak familiarly with you,
> or laugh with you, or visit in your house and go to work with you?[19]

The silenced soldiers in their graves, the civilian dead, the scarred earth, and the living "whose souls have been disfigured" by war beseech us to answer.

---

18 Seville Statement on Violence, Spain, 1986, UNESCO

19 Wendell Berry, "To a Siberian Woodsman," *The Selected Poems of Wendell Berry*

The Joy Inside

The Call to Joy

I begin most days with a walk, often in the woods. While my dog, Zuki, follows her nose, dashing about, I list my blessings in a litany of gratitude. On the days when brilliant blue sky frames the unfurling leaves, it's impossible not to revel in the grace of the world. The woods are such a lovely antidote to human news. The way life teems among branches, fallen or standing, the scrub brush chattering around my ankles.

On Monday's walk, overcome with delight at the shape of my life now, I recalled how I used to feel immobilized by the vast suffering in the world. How, I wondered, could I go about my plentiful life in the presence of so much need? In the midst of my fretting about what I could not do, could not solve, and could not save, a friend asked, "What would it mean to answer the call to joy?"

I wasn't sure I understood the question so I wrote it on a memo board. Daily, I pondered how my friend had phrased her question. She didn't say, "What would it mean to be happy?" She didn't ask what it would mean to be content or satisfied. She asked what it would mean to *answer the call* to joy.

The language of call is religious: the sound of the cosmos itself summoning us to something important, taking up a particular vocation or form of service. And since answering a call suggests a religious experience, I began to wonder how that relates to joy. What makes it a calling? Is joy a religious experience? And how do we recognize joy in the midst of a world blighted by suffering, in a culture preoccupied with happiness?

The thirteenth-century Sufi poet Rumi writes: "Keep knocking and the joy inside will eventually open a window and look to see who's there." This suggests joy dwells deep within. It doesn't float on the surface, like oil atop a rain-slickened road. It doesn't come free in the cereal box or with a scratch card for the lottery. It takes its own time, and sometimes the path it travels tastes of sorrow, or regret.

For many of us, true joy arises in the shadow of difficulty or at least challenge. While pleasure may derive from momentary sensation, and happiness may bloom out of satisfaction or mirth, joy travels through fertile darkness to reach the light. It has a depth that resonates. Perhaps that's one way we can recognize it: by the vibration we feel at the core of our being.

To feel that vibration can be its own joy, particularly in the presence of suffering. On my Monday walk as I offered a prayer for all the beings in peril, I contemplated the magnitude of life. Gazillions of beings—how every moment some tender shoot gets stepped on, insects get crushed. (At the second I typed that line I looked down and saw a tick crawling on my keyboard cable and sadly, I squished it. The universe underscores the veracity of its truths.) Every minute somewhere on earth people and animals die horrible deaths; rivers and plants and marine creatures choke on our toxins. Suffering is indeed the marrow, and if the great Buddhist teacher Thich Nhat Hanh is right, that suffering engenders compassion and, thus, who would want to live in a world without it? It makes no sense to pray that all suffering cease. Even if we want it to, it won't. But it occurs to me that we are called to notice the suffering and in so doing, in that sharp intake of breath, the sigh we emit in the face of suffering becomes part of the song.

Joy is not a solution to suffering, but it is a response.

To quote Rumi again, "An eye is meant to see things. The soul is here for its own joy."

Over the last twenty-plus years, I have taught and volunteered in prisons. Buildings with little or no natural light. Drab monochrome, layers of frustration cemented by anger, sometimes encased in despair. I have passed through the electronically operated doors into concrete slab rooms, bearing as much color as I could. Paper, fabric, words. Any medium would do. When I taught at the women's prison in New Hampshire in the early nineties, I invited women to tell stories or to find themselves in someone else's. We studied literature and change, and in moments unobserved, we abetted transformation. One afternoon I asked the women in class what it would mean for them to seek happiness; one responded by saying, "They hate for us to be happy in here." It's hard to be happy in prison. Very little merriment. Few sources of pleasure. Restricted access to comfort or solace. But the women in that class taught me about joy.

Another day, a group of women gathered with my friend Jen, who'd brought in plaster masks and lots of art supplies. Markers, paint, beads, sequins, forbidden feathers. The superintendent came in, pulled me aside, and threatened: "If I find one feather in anyone's cell, you're never coming back." As soon as she left I said, "Is she afraid someone might tickle herself?" and Gigi quickly answered, "That's exactly right."

In an institution intended to dehumanize, fifteen women decorated masks that revealed themselves. In telling each other about the masks they made, they inhabited a space made precious by their being. They weren't allowed to keep the masks, but they made them anyway, because the process of creating them gave those women a way to answer the call to joy.

One need not enter a prison to find joy, but one need not confine prison to the kind with razor wire and correctional officers. Consider the prisons we may inhabit: shame, guilt, dishonesty, self-doubt, addiction, unresolved anger. Someone else's *shoulds*. Achievement defined by another's values. Believing joy belongs to someone else. Rumi instructs us to "Become the sky / Take an ax to that prison wall—escape / Walk out like someone suddenly born into color. / Do it now."

Keep knocking.

After a long day of university teaching, I would drive to the women's prison, often weary, sometimes depressed, on a spiritual journey I did not yet recognize. There, women taught me how to find freedom within constraint. Women who laughed with me and shared the intimacy of silence. Women who read aloud and let themselves feel the vibration of collective voices. Women who hung their vibrant masks on the classroom bulletin board as if to say, "Walk out like someone suddenly born into color." Seeing that wall of masks and knowing what went into making them and leaving them behind filled my throat with tears. One night, under a waxing moon, I scribbled as I drove home:

> The silver throated orchid
> grows sideways
> reaching toward light,
> undaunted by low ceilings,
> it sings out the window
> to sweet peas climbing by,
> trailing arpeggios across the roof
> serenading the great orange moon
> rising into sky.
> Like a cake pulled too early,
> the top edge of the moon is gone,
> sweetness collecting in the dark.
> Dig your hands deep
> and plant your own lullaby.
> Harvest your dreams
> and sleep well
> knowing what can flourish
> in the slice of invisible moon.

What spilled out as a poem came from the wellspring of joy I had witnessed and experienced, a joy that answered the knocking and opened the barred window to see who was there.

I used to question whether it's right in a world so ravaged to experience joy. Considering all the travail and heartbreak, contemplating what it means to read *Bon Appétit* in a world where tens of thousands die each day of hunger and a billion people lack clean water. When I hear of yet another senseless death, it's easy to cast aside joy. But then I remember what the dead and dying ask of the living is to embrace life, to let the sigh become part of the song.

Inside the fullness of life, the comic and tragic, the complex and breathtakingly simple co-exist. Joy is part of the paradox. New lives enter the world as others lay dying. During winter, when trees appear bare, inside they are re-inventing spring. The devastation of earthquakes and tornadoes, the machinations of war, the assault of terror anywhere insist that we listen harder for the vibration of joy. Perhaps that's why I love the woods, where I feel the hum of existence, the living and the dying commingled, inviting me into the thrum of being.

On my walks I engage of a litany of gratitude because, frankly, I am overcome with the breadth of my good fortune. Understanding the way my life—and perhaps yours—reflects the gift of feeling held. Even in the uncertainty that all life involves, some lives, like mine, center on trust.

We don't enter this building warily, looking over our shoulders thinking someone might gun us down. We don't suspect newcomers of infiltrating to turn us in to the secret police. We don't live under tyranny. We don't dodge landmines or roving gangs of militia as some do. We have the good fortune to be open to the possibility of grace, to lead lives that afford the possibility of trust, even faith.

For years I have spoken of a benevolent universe. The benevolence isn't tied to a lack of suffering; it arises out of a demanding joy. Joy that bears the cost of mindfulness: the awareness that all life entwines, all sorrow springs from the same cosmic pool; hardship and hazard anywhere affect the thrum of life everywhere.

Our joy affects the whole planet, too.

Recently, I spent the day at in the medium security unit of the men's prison in Shirley, Massachusetts, co-facilitating a workshop on Alternatives to Violence. In an exercise called Concentric Circles we paired up and had two minutes each to answer the question, "What's something you've let go of in the last year?" Immediately I answered, "Self-imposed constraints." Leaving our self-made prisons frees us to answer the call to joy.

What makes joy demanding is that leaving prison takes courage. Any incarcerated person will tell you that. After Moses led the Israelites out of Egypt, they reached a point where they wanted to go back. But if we are willing to take an ax to the prison walls we construct, if we are willing in the midst of suffering and grief to respond to our soul's stirring, if we allow ourselves to feel the thrum of life vibrating within, we can answer the call to joy.

While hope calls us back from the brink of despair by inviting us to imagine a different time, reality or place, joy summons us to inhabit *this* moment, already ripe. Joy calls to us in our uncertainty and offers itself within the very garden of our limitation. It does not depend on material possessions or success. It does even require happiness. It emerges when we risk revealing ourselves by naming our masks. It relies on our capacity to connect with what matters, to notice the pulse of existence that binds us to all being.

This is why joy is a religious experience. It not about singularity of a religious tradition or institution. Joy cares not if you are Sufi, pagan, humanist, Jew. It cares not if you are Christian or Hindu or Buddhist or animist. It doesn't even care if you say, "I'm spiritual, not religious." It cares only that you keep knocking. That you engage with life on life's terms, that you take an ax to the prison wall that confines your soul. Joy expresses life's longing for itself.

"Keep knocking," Rumi writes, "and the joy inside will eventually open a window and look to see who's there." Will it be you?

What Is Worth Pursuing?

A colleague of mine at Keene State College is teaching a section of the same course I teach, Integrative Thinking and Writing. There are some forty sections of this course, each with a specific theme or topic chosen by the instructor. Students choose the section that interests them or fits in their schedule. Like me, Alice has two sections, each with its own theme. One is "Death and Dying," the other "The Pursuit of Happiness." Guess that about covers it. I was sufficiently intrigued by Alice's topics that we got together over coffee to talk about them. There is no shortage of students interested in a writing course on death and dying, and according to Alice, the students in that section seem more engaged than the ones pursuing happiness.

As you all know, much has been researched and written about happiness. To name just a few recent books:

Climb Your Stairway to Heaven: The 9 Habits of Maximum Happiness

The Art of Happiness: A Handbook for Living (by the Dalai Lama, no less)

The Pursuit of Happiness: Discovering the Pathway to Fulfillment, Well-Being, and Enduring Personal Joy

Happiness: Lessons from a New Science

And lastly, by one of the foremost psychologists studying happiness, Martin Seligman, *Authentic Happiness: Using the New Positive Psychology to Realize Your Potential for Lasting Fulfillment.*

Interestingly enough, my colleague uses none of these as her course text. Instead she chose Barbara Ehrenreich's book, *Bright-Sided: How Positive Thinking Is Undermining America.*

Apparently, happiness has its limits and even its encroachments.

What compelled me most about my conversation with Alice were her own questions: Is there something of more value to us as humans than happiness? Is contentment the same as happiness or is it deeper? Why *is* happiness so darn important? Is it what we should be pursuing?

Obviously, it is not necessary for the propagation of the species; nor does our happiness insure planetary well-being. If anything, what we conflate with happiness—the allure of more, immediate gratification, and unbridled appetites—does more harm to the earth than good.

So what then is the value of happiness? Is it reducible to a simple-minded positivism available to anyone who harnesses the power of positive thinking? Is it an attitude, brought on perhaps by gratitude? Or is it deeper than that? More than a state of prolonged pleasure? Is happiness a state of contentment brought about by attitude and achievement? Does it involve a level of accomplishment that requires a modicum of opportunity that must be guaranteed by the state? Is that why its pursuit is essential to the American Declaration of Independence? Is it what compelled the Dalai Lama to collaborate with leading neuroscientist Richard Davidson?

Using brain imagery to track what happens to a mind happily engrossed in meditation, scientists can now "promote resilience and happiness and other positive qualities of the mind through enhanced training and mental exercises."

Some psychologists posit happiness as a state of well-being. Davidson defines it as "a combination of positive emotional states, including contentment, satisfaction, pleasure and joy ... associated with actively embracing the world and being fully engaged."

What happens to happiness if it resides in the state of embrace—our capacity, willingness, desire to embrace the world, and in turn, be engaged?

Perhaps this is what shifts happiness from a psychological to a spiritual experience. Or perhaps this is what directs us to our deepest values.

But precisely because happiness gets co-opted by movements of prosperity and positivism, it may be worthwhile to take up

Alice's question, to determine whether the pursuit of attentiveness and engagement rank up there with life and liberty.

In his book *Climb Your Stairway to Heaven: The 9 Habits of Maximum Happiness*, David Leonhardt identifies elements of attentiveness and engagement such as seizing the day, counting blessings, and spreading joy, though he also devotes a fair amount of word-space to good old-fashioned self-focused positive thinking.

But in a world so clearly filled with suffering—the atrocities that repeat themselves in each generation, the rampant inequity in the distribution and allocation of resources, and a mindset that encourages us to perceive everything from trees to talent to terrapins as resources to maximize—do attentiveness and engagement require more than positive thoughts and stress reduction?

What does attentiveness ask?

One day, in the midst of my own happiness—let's call it a state of well-being I asked a wise and Buddhist-flavored counselor. Why is it I get to be so happy and experience joy and comfort while so many beings suffer?

Karma, she answered. We don't know what their karma requires of them but yours requires that you bear witness to their suffering, that you notice and acknowledge it.

In short, my karma demands my attentiveness and engagement. Apparently how I engage is an open and endless question. Must I, must we, follow the trail of tears to hotspots and war zones, disasters and landscapes of desolation? Some of us do feel called to foreign soil. And of some us, myself included, adhere to Wendell Berry's maxim that we must respond where history has placed us. Here, now, where my paws are. This is the realm of my influence, the specificity of my embrace.

As I immersed myself in the engagement with you that entails writing sermons, I paused long enough to take my dog for a walk in the woods. We are lucky to live next to many acres of young forest where Zuki prowls, happily unleashed. (If I know nothing about human happiness, I imagine canine bliss as the moment the leash snaps off the collar and Zuki darts unimpeded into the woods.) As I ambled along the trail I heard the rustle of dogs: not one, more. As Zuki cantered toward me I saw what looked like a tawny shepherd followed by a brindled reddish-grayish-yellowish one in pursuit. They were, of course, coyotes and as I watched to see what they would do—hoping there would not be aggression in the mix—the coyotes noticed me and slunk away. God, they were beautiful, and without thinking, I muttered a prayer aloud that they be kept well, that they survive the winter, unharmed by hunters. And then I thought of the deer that roam the forest, the ones who will be inevitably eaten so that the coyotes stay alive. Zuki and I have come upon the barest remains of a downed deer, the ground cover of fur, the elegant, fleshless spine, the partial skull. No beauty there, other than perhaps the cycle of woodland life unintruded upon by humans. The moment with the beautiful coyotes and my beautiful dog, similar in build and size but for her sleek and complete blackness, summoned me to embrace the awe of wildness with its inherent pain.

It invites, lo, insists that I engage wholeheartedly with the encounter: that is to say the heart that beats desire for coyote well-being, and the heart that beats breathless coming upon a carpet of fur emptied of its being.

Thus, to engage fully doesn't always feel like happiness. To engage with life when grief burgles the house and redecorates, hanging drapes so opaque it seems impossible for any light to get through. Surely that is not happiness, but the resulting impulse to get out of the house or hunker further down signals a pulse. Embrace is not always an expression of joy, a sign of affection. Sometimes it denotes relief—in dogspeak, embrace often involves teeth, sometimes playfully, sometimes not.

A combination of attentiveness and engagement, embrace is the state of beholding the world as we are held by it. Neuroscientists and Buddhist monks recognize it as a kind of oneness with being.

Instead of pursuing happiness, why not pursue the notion of embrace, noticing what we notice and attending to its fullness?

David Stendl-Rast posits the antidote to exhaustion isn't rest; it is wholeheartedness. The antidote to discontent might be wholeheartedness as well.

On Being Found

Reading: Luke 12:13-21

Someone in the crowd said to him, "Teacher, tell my brother to divide the family inheritance with me." But he said to him, "Friend, who set me to be a judge or arbitrator over you?" And he said to them, "Take care! Be on your guard against all kinds of greed; for one's life does not consist in the abundance of possessions." Then he told them a parable: "The land of a rich man produced abundantly. And he thought to himself, What should I do, for I have no place to store my crops? Then he said, 'I will do this: I will pull down my barns and build larger ones, and there I will store all my grains and my goods. And I will say to my soul, Soul, you have ample goods laid up for many years; relax, eat, drink, be merry.' But God said to him, 'You fool! This very night of your life is being demanded of you. And the things you have prepared, whose will they be?' So it is with those who store up treasures for themselves but are not rich toward God."

Before going to divinity school, I read a book called *Searching for God at Harvard*. Shortly thereafter, my minister gave me another book called *Finding God at Harvard*. In my three years at Harvard Divinity School, a place many assume to be profoundly secular, I developed a whole new appreciation for God. I entered theological school as a panentheist, one for whom God is in all being. God did not denote *a* being but rather *beingness*. The sum and thrum of all life's processes and moments. Here's what changed for me about God while I studied at Harvard: I started saying the word. Not intentionally. It slipped out, almost against my will. During my ministerial internship, waiting for a traffic light at a busy interchange, I handed a homeless woman bearing a cardboard sign a five-dollar bill and heard myself say, "God bless." Never before would I have imagined those words exiting my mouth. The phrase had always sounded too easy; it conjured politicians and religious conservatives promoting short-sighted, small-hearted policies, closing their remarks with "God bless."

But in that moment I put the money in the woman's hand and looked her in the eye, she thanked me so sincerely that I felt ashamed of a world so imbalanced that I got to be the good schnook because I had five dollars to spare and the inclination to offer it. How could I not call on God, on the presence of all that is holy to bless that encounter, to bless that woman so obviously struggling within a political and economic system predicated on capital, not care? And how could I fail to ask for blessing in that moment when I could have so easily kept my window rolled up against another's suffering? Summoning God was linguistically expedient—one short syllable instead of "the holiness that permeates creation" or "Spirit of Life" or "The Benevolent Universe"—and it involved something more.

The dozen years before divinity school, I talked to trees, prayed with my arms around them. I preferred the word "divine" to the word "God." *God* with its hard consonant sounded limited and limiting, whereas *divine* with its long vowel sounded open and flowing like my sense of the holy. But from the day I encountered the woman standing on the median strip, I have experienced more often and more closely the presence of God. Here's what changed: using the word sparks an immediacy, a palpable presence of the holy beyond my beloved trees.

In my first-year div school seminar, I was going on devoutly about trees when a classmate said, "I don't get it. The trees I know are scrawny and leafless, stuck in a piece of cement."

For the first time I understood that the metaphors and language we use to describe and apprehend the divine depend on our location: social *and* geographic. Just as my classmate's experience framed her question to me, experience informed the sincere if naïve question to a different classmate named

Stephanie, an African-American woman who considered Unitarian Universalism before choosing Episcopalianism. How, I asked, had African Americans sustained belief in God during centuries of slavery without liberation. There we sat in Cambridge, Massachusetts, in a tony chocolate shop, the din of chatter rising. Stephanie leaned forward so I could hear above the hum of privileged patrons and said, "Leaf, who else would we believe in? It's not like black folks could count on *people* to do the right thing."

Years later, I heard the eminent African-American theologian James Cone in an interview with Bill Moyers, discussing God's presence and relevance. Dr. Cone said,

> "As long as you know that you are a human being and nobody can take that away from you, then God is that reality in your life that enables you to know that.... There is a spirit deep in you that nobody can take away from you because it's a creation that God gave to you."

Later in the interview, Bill Moyers asks James Cone, "Do you believe God is love?"

Dr. Cone replies, "Yes, I believe God is love," to which Mr. Moyers counters, "I would have a hard time believing God is love if I were a black man....Where was God during the four hundred years of slavery?"

Apparently I wasn't the only well-meaning white person to wonder. To both Bill Moyers and me, Dr. Cone responds:

> You are looking at it from the perspective of those who win. You have to see it from the perspective of those who have no power. In fact, God is love because it's that power in your life that lets you know you can resist the definitions that other people are being—placing on you. And you sort of say, sure, nobody knows the trouble I've seen. Nobody knows my sorrow. Sure, there is slavery. Sure, there is lynching, segregation.
>
> But, glory, hallelujah. Now, that glory hallelujah is the fact

that there is a humanity and a spirit that nobody can kill. And as long as you know that, you will resist. That was the power of the civil rights movement. That was the power of those who kept marching even though the odds are against you. How do you keep going when you don't have the battle tanks, when you don't have the guns? When you don't have the military power? When you have nothing? How do you keep going? How do you know that you are a human being? You know because there's a power that transcends all of that.... God is that power. That power that enables you to resist.[20]

The God of Luke and James Cone summons us to justice. God is *Ruach*, the Breath that animates beyond the body's capacity to inhale. I spent nine days in Mexico with Benedictine nuns who took us to meet impoverished *campesinos* to make Liberation Theology come alive. That's where I learned what James Cone is talking about. People's lives are ground into dust by poverty and exploitation but each morning, the people rise—filled with the power to resist—and they identify that power with a short sturdy syllable: God.

Allen Callahan, a New Testament scholar and a Baptist minister, gave a class lecture at the request of the Living Wage Campaign, standing on a wooden platform in the middle of Harvard Yard, to show solidarity with the workers. Professor Callahan exhorted, "To constrain someone to work against their interests outrages God."

There is power in the syllable, the power of *Ruach*, the power of resistance, the power that fills the lungs and restores dignity when other humans are hellbent on stripping it.

There is an *oomph* to God.

For me, God conjures a mystery and a presence calling in the darkness "This very night your life is being demanded of you. And the things you have prepared, whose will they be?' So it is

20 www.pbs.org/moyers/journal/11232007/transcript1.html

with those who store up treasures for themselves but are not rich toward God."

The same voice blurts out "God bless" to a woman in need whether she stands in the middle of a busy highway or rolls up the window to contemplate building a bigger barn. God is the presence that will not stand idly by as we imperil the planet and oppress each other. God dwells in the mighty winds and the torrential rains, in the heartbreak of people sopping up their lives, in the fury of mourners and the despair of those who have made them mourn. God dwells in the words that summon us to love that mysterious and perhaps familiar presence that calls us out of selfishness into the Selfhood of all.

Frederick May Eliot, one of the most influential Unitarians in the twentieth century, though a theist himself, responded positively to the Humanist movement that helped shape our denomination. Eliot understood that the word "God" could be problematic—loaded with baggage—yet he also knew the word, like all words, functioned as symbol. For Frederick May Eliot, symbols afforded people a way to come into contact with religious reality. Eliot described his belief in God as an affirmation of a moral imperative and a sense of purpose reflected in a rationally ordered universe.

Eliot wrote,

> We need somehow to get our basic convictions so deep down into our lives that they will govern our actions at those moments when there is no time to think, and the best way to do that is to give them expression in symbolic forms which are colorful and rich in emotional appeal. We need symbols that will reach down deep into our souls and make their power felt in the innermost recesses of our personality. ... The word "God" is such a symbol.

It matters not if God is provable. It matters that we remember all metaphor springs from the ground of our being. Our questions and our answers are of service when they bind us to each other, reminding us the self arises in context and connection. To forget is to cleave from wholeness.

The day I encountered the woman asking for help on the highway, God spilled out of my mouth, a verb. In that moment I realized God doesn't pause like a bowler waiting for the ball to shoot out of the return tunnel after the first toss down the alley. God pulses in the momentum of the ball traveling the darkness. God sighs in the crack of pins and the disappointment inherent in a gutter ball. God gleams in the polished wood floor and floats in free radical cells and limbic neurons, and in our waiting.

For me, God has become the code word for the wholeness of life that renders meaning.

The Days of Awe

These are the Days of Awe. In the Jewish liturgical calendar, the ten days starting with Rosh Hashanah and concluding with Yom Kippur, which begins tonight at sundown, are set aside as a time of reflection, reconciliation, and atonement. While Yom Kippur focuses on returning to right relation with God, the Days of Awe designate time to take personal inventory, to make amends, to seek or offer forgiveness—as a way of restoring right relation with others.

Of all the Jewish holidays I grew up with, the Days of Awe and Yom Kippur engage me most deeply, perhaps because the spiritual work of these ten days reflects the spiritual work of twelve-step recovery I try to engage in all year. There is something powerful in the practice of setting ten days aside to recollect, to stop short and reconsider what may have seemed fine at the time but wasn't so kosher. And to paraphrase an old ad for rye bread, you don't have to be Jewish to find value in the Days of Awe or Yom Kippur.

To realign ourselves with one another, with the ground of our being, to return to a state of at-one-ment requires that we pause, breathe, listen to our literal breath in concert with the Breath of the Universe, and hear the places we lose the rhythm. For it is only in being able to recognize those moments that we can right them.

During my banjo lesson this week, the teacher instructed me to listen to the rhythm of the song, to hear the length of an eighth-note, a quarter-note, to hear how the bum-ditty strum compares in duration to the melody note. Banjo is a rhythm instrument, one of the few used to play melody and rhythm together. Not easy, he told me. But instructive, for as I learn to hear the rhythm, which doesn't come easily to me, it's a great metaphor for the kind of daily listening a mindful life requires. It is not enough to learn which notes to hit or when to strum. I need to learn how long each note lasts, how to substitute strumming a chord for melody notes without losing the rhythm. Be it music lessons or life lessons, the universe instructs us in the importance of paying attention.

These Days of Awe have occasioned a review of the moments when I have failed to notice the nuance, favoring instead a dualism not unlike my saying, "Gee, I hit the right note and strummed when the notation directed. Isn't that good enough? "And the universe whispers back, "No, not really. Try again. Look for patterns in relation to the notes. Listen to the sound of your action in relation to the needs of others."

I've never thought of God as the great banjo teacher tuning up in the heavens, but I see how the divine enters into the daily practices and pleasures of our lives. The introspection of the last week and a half yielded fruitful truths. We needn't enter a synagogue or church, *daven* (the Orthodox habit of thrice-daily prayer), or kneel before the altar to engage the holy within and beyond. We can access the sacred in our life by paying attention. As Simone Weil so aptly put it: "absolute, unmixed attention is a form of prayer." The lessons life teaches us come in all forms. The invitation to realign ourselves with each other, the earth, the Source of All Being comes in myriad ways. It is our responsibility to answer.

Recently I sat with my wise friend Kimberly, a spiritual director by nature as much as training, who asked, "How does God see you?" Quickly, too quickly, I replied, "I don't know how God sees me. You'd have to ask God." Gently, firmly, the way a parent might propel a child on a swing, Kimberly said, "You know."

I thought for a moment about my daily walks in the woods with my dog, Zuki, how I talk to God down the trail and try to listen on the way back. The operative word is *try.* It's a challenge to quiet the internal chatter, to still my mind long enough to hear the wise trees, to match my footsteps with the rhythm to which we all belong. Harmonizing with the Breath of Life is easier described than done, but the daily ritual of walking prayer forms an image God sees of me moving deliberately, expressing gratitude, attempting to listen, paying attention, wandering, returning, over and over, yearning to stay in step even as I stray.

All of us get caught in life's brambles. We stumble on a root or lose our way. An unusual plant catches our eye and pulls us off course. A trail bends left and we go right, or wrong. Sometimes we catch ourselves, and sometimes we don't; but my sense is that the universe, or God, or that which enfolds and claims us as its own, holds us as we career off the path and nudges us back toward the path—as long as we pay attention. A loving nudge can feel like a bullying push if we ignore the context. For me, the nudges have often come in a form that felt a lot more like being summoned to the principal's office than being happily launched into the air, but I have finally come to understand that God sees what it takes to get my attention. I'm just one of those people who occasionally gets so transfixed by the golden light filtering through leaves that I fail to notice what skitters around my feet.

Perhaps you have felt a sharp tug as the divine snaps you to attention. The Days of Awe instruct us not to resist but rather to yield to the intervention. To offer ourselves up to the lessons, to meet them more than halfway as they wend toward us.

I recall such a lesson that took place in a Harvard Square bookstore. I heard my name as I was browsing and looked around. Seeing no one I knew I assumed I had misheard what wasn't my name and went back to browsing. And then, at the end of the aisle, a young woman appeared I had not seen for several years. Someone whose feelings I had trounced on not out of malice or ill-intent, but carelessness and ignorance. She had vanished from the horizon and though I had thought of her many times over the years, and wished I could have apologized, I had tucked my regret in one of many pockets full of remorse. But then there she was and she had called my name when she could have ignored me. I probably would not have seen her in that crowded store.

We spoke briefly. She told me of her brother's suicide. I told her how sorry I was about that and so many other things. I apologized for hurting her feelings, for being so unaware. She gave me her address and we began to correspond. I of course wanted to instantly reconnect and be friends, but she was more cautious and insisted we write and reacquaint ourselves slowly. I needed to earn her trust.

In time, I did.

What we get are little resolutions, small reconciliations that revive us. We get no assurance that the path we tread won't suddenly appear to vanish. We get no guarantee that cruelty or loss or unbearable sadness won't come our way. We are issued no promises that we won't stumble into the puckerbrush or careen down a rocky slope.

What we get are opportunities to come round right. To be lifted once again, to participate in restoration. Sometimes that requires being humbled by the sound of a previously unrecognized truth emerging. Sometimes it means the apology we seek is in fact an apology we need to offer. Sometimes the grievance belong to all parties, not just the one who complains.

The process of discernment can take many forms; each requires attentiveness at the root. The ways we atone, seek to redress those instances of rupture, begin with quieting ourselves, turning inward to take inventory, to review what we have done and what we have failed to do. The resentments we carry, the bruises still tender, invite us to consider our part: our actions, their effects, intended or inadvertent. The Days of Awe summon us to first face ourselves, in full light and shadow, to probe the crevices, the nooks where dust bunnies gather and old hurts smolder. The Days of Awe call upon us to turn to another, to set our gaze on those to whom we belong, because our humanity is shared. To focus our *absolute unmixed attention* on the felt truth of another's experience, and in so doing, reckon with ourselves. Lastly, Yom

Kippur brings the process full circle by making a space to realign with God, or the wholeness within. To step back far enough to gain perspective, to see how we appear to the divine. How does the wholeness of life, the ground of our being, perceive us? What will it take to bring ourselves into alignment with that view?

My friend Sarah asked me why they are called the Days of Awe. Herein lies an answer. To bring oneself into alignment is an awesome task. Awe lies at the heart of Jewish tradition. The awe induced by the sight of a burning bush that is not consumed by fire; the awe of standing on holy ground; the awe of God passing over yet not revealing a face. The Days of Awe are so named because if we engage with them, and the spiritual work they invite, they can realign in a way no less stunning than brambles alight with the fire of God.

The Roses of Guadalupe

This third Sunday of Advent falls this year on December twelfth, the Feast of our Lady of Guadalupe, a day when thousands of Mexican pilgrims make their way to the Basilica of Guadalupe, many traveling by bicycle and some arriving on their knees to pay homage to the Virgin.

I visited the Basilica about a month after the feast day in 2001; still hundreds of pilgrims filed by me on their knees. Thousands gathered to view the displayed piece of fabric bearing the image of Mary found by a peasant named Juan Diego this day in 1531.

The Benedictine nuns who took us to the shrine told us the miraculous origin of the cloth.

A peasant named Juan Diego was traveling from his home village to Mexico City when he came upon a young woman surrounded in light who instructed him in the local language of Nahuatl to build a church in her honor. Juan Diego recognized the woman as the Virgin Mother. He hurried to tell the bishop, who instructed him to return to the site and ask the woman for a sign proving her identity. So off Juan went and when he found her, he asked for a sign and she told him to go up the rocky hill and gather flowers. And though it was winter he found roses everywhere. Guadalupe herself arranged the flowers in his cloak and bade him not to move them until he reached the bishop. Juan Diego returned to the bishop and when he opened his cloak, the flowers fell to the floor and in their place a glowing figure of her appeared on the cloth where the petals had been.

It is that image on Juan Diego's cloak that hangs in the basilica.

The nuns explain Guadalupe's name really means "the one who protects us from the ones who eat us," undoubtedly a reference to the Spanish conquistadors Indians like Juan Diego faced. "She is mestiza," says Sister Fatima. "She welcomes the children of Spanish fathers and indigenous mothers," inviting the blended into her maternal embrace.

On my winter visit, roses bloomed in the gardens of the nuns just as they bloomed before Juan Diego.

In the Christian liturgical calendar, certain colors correspond with each Sunday in Advent. Because Advent begins like Lent as a time of penitence and fasting, altars first feature purple, a color associated with both penitence and royalty, but by the third week they shift to bright blue to signify the night sky that will herald the rising star or the waters of life associated with creation, *or they feature rose* to reflect the joy inherent in the coming birth.

This year the third Sunday of Advent falls on December twelfth, the day Mexicans honor Guadalupe, who chose as a sign of her authenticity roses abloom out of season on a rocky hillside.

There is a way the Spirit alights today no less wondrously or mysteriously than it appeared before Juan Diego. No less wondrously or mysteriously than it appeared to Mary herself when the angel Gabriel announced to her she would carry a son.

It is easy for folks who prefer a more rational approach to life than religious miracles portend to dismiss the relevance of such stories, but the nine days I spent in Mexico a decade ago with the nuns taught me otherwise and summon me to heed the message of this time of year. So on this Mexican high holy day, it feels fitting to recount my experience, not with an apparition of Guadalupe, but an incarnation of her that appeared in the form of Benedictine sisters in their modest blue skirts and white blouses, cinnamon skin, and dark eyes closer to the color of a Middle Eastern Mary than the paler versions we know.

Benedictines, whether monks or nuns, follow the Rule of Benedict, a set of directions for monastic life written in the sixth century by Benedict of Nursia, whose wisdom shaped Western monasticism. Ten months a year, the good sisters at *Las Misioneras*

Guadalupanas de Cristo Rey welcome visitors from the United States for a program called "Faith/Hospitality Experience in Latin America." For nine days, people like me are given the chance to experience Benedictine hospitality. For Benedictines, each guest is a representative of Christ.

Upon our arrival at the retreat center, several nuns rush out to greet us. Each one offers a big hug and says in English, "Welcome home." In our rooms, much more spacious than the ones the nuns live in, we each find a vase of flowers next to a hand-lettered card with our name and another "welcome." In each bathroom is a bottle of purified water. In our three daily chapel services, the nuns provide readings in English and play tapes of U.S. monks singing. In the dining room there are Oreos and mashed potatoes. Hot dogs and grilled cheese. Evidence abounds of their effort to make us feel at home.

Year-round the nuns work with the poor of Cuernavaca. Part of their mission is to educate us about that reality. Eighty percent of Mexico's people live in poverty. Illiteracy and malnutrition contribute to vast underemployment. We listen to guest speakers and watch a twenty-year-old video about the hidden Holocaust of Guatemala—a civil war where 135,000 people died. We meet survivors of that war who have settled in Mexico. Every day, we visit children and adults who labor to subsist. On a dirt walkway just over the hill from the retreat center, we chat with four women, shovels in hand, creating a road from a heap of gravel. Another day, we visit four families in The Station, a cramped, non-arable swath of government land where thirty thousand squatters live in dwellings constructed from scraps. In the homes we enter, little light shines in. There are no windows amidst the corrugated metal and stone. Dust. Rats. Bare light bulbs. Outhouses. Strips of cloth functioning as doors. Conditions that mirror the encampments of poor blacks who lived a mile from my childhood home in Tennessee, reminiscent of lives lived in cardboard box villages and in subway tunnels. Each foray led by the nuns a billboard for the prophet Jeremiah who wrote: *Woe to him who builds his house by unrighteousness, and his upper rooms by injustice; that makes his neighbors work for nothing, and does not give them their wages.*

The good sisters aim to churn our consciousness by exposing us to harsh realities. They want us to consider the ways we spend our disposable income and think twice before supporting NAFTA; but it is the nuns themselves, voices soft and laughter keen, who stir my soul beyond measure. It is their oft-repeated melodies sung on or off key, in praise of a God that restores their hope daily and calls them to serve by accompanying them as they do.

In Cuernavaca as I read aloud the poetry of Mary Oliver each day as part of my morning meditation, sitting outside among lavish winter roses, apricot and ivory, I realize why the people I meet there need the Lady of Guadalupe, a mestiza incarnation of Mary who fuses indigenous religion with Christianity in a way that makes sense to conquered people. As I walk to 7 a.m. chapel, marveling at the roses and hibiscus, the palette of sky as the sun transforms it, I experience the divine in Mary Oliver's images and the scent of flora, in the colors and texture and infinite wisdom of the universe. And as soon as I sit down in the chapel, careful to select a seat that permits me to gaze out the picture window at the rising sun and the reflection of the candle in the foliage on the hill so that I peer into a burning bush, the nuns sing praises to El Senor, to a human incarnation of God who suffers with the poor. As the sound of the nuns singing psalms in Spanish fills my ear, I feel the presence of the God they invoke.

Up until that moment, I have experienced a sense of the divine through poetry. My realm of the sacred: magnificent trees. Not surprising for a person who lives in a wooded landscape where the trees have room to grow like spires. But there in the small room filled with the good sisters of Guadalupe, my horizon of the sacred expands.

The sisters faithfully bow to the consecrated host in a glass box that hangs from the chapel ceiling, wafers made holy, they tell me, by blessings of the priest. And at that moment, I see as clearly as Juan Diego did the presence of holiness. Not in the host consecrated by the priest, but in the welcome consecrated by nuns who embody the risen spirit in their radical hospitality, their tireless pursuit of justice, their unsung labor—they emanate a God that before, I would have only seen present in the petals of rose light that bloom on the chapel wall at evening prayer.

It is the nuns who instruct me why it is that, as lovely as their flowers are, what ultimately stirs Juan Diego and centuries of his descendents is the image of a mestiza Mary welcoming them as graciously as the Virgin accepts the fullness of her womb, a pregnancy she does not choose. The message Mary imparts is that within each of us the divine gestates and comes to light when we, as courageously as she does, welcome the unbidden. When we heed the great Sufi poet Rumi, who writes: "Be grateful for whoever comes / because each has been sent / as a guide from beyond."

I keep replaying the words of sister Ramona telling me that after we depart, they will clean our rooms, launder the linens, re-make the beds. "This is our work," she says.

I think of my wise congregant who tells me our job is to stay in our joy. And I think of Guadalupe instructing a peasant to gather flowers where he least expects them. I recall gazing up in the Basilica at that cloth, centuries old, beholding the image of a woman radiating light, arms extended in welcome. I recall the sight of men and women walking on their knees across an acre of concrete in humility and praise, traveling like the legendary wise men to pay homage to "the one who protects them from the ones who will eat [them]."

We rarely believe it is the unknown that will protect us. We don't associate the unbidden or unexpected with what saves us. Usually, we meet the unknown with apprehension or run the other way. But on the feast day of Guadalupe, the third Sunday of Advent, may the color of roses, the color of joy, remind us of flowers that bloom when and where we least expect. May we, like Juan Diego, see holiness on the hillside, and like Mary, feel it stirring within.

Communion

Today is Easter and once again I welcome the invitation and the challenge to find meaning in Easter as a Jewish Unitarian Universalist. In the Christian tradition, Easter centers on the Passion narrative, which begins as Jesus enters Jerusalem to celebrate Passover. In the gospel of Matthew: "While they were eating, Jesus took a loaf of bread, and after blessing it, gave it to the disciples, and said, 'Take, eat; this is my body'" (Matt 26:26).

Now for those of us who don't celebrate the Eucharist, or "Lord's Supper," or Holy Communion as it is known, the phrase, "Take, eat, this is my body" may at worst offend, and at best, confound. It's useful, however, not to dismiss this line. Judaism and Unitarian Universalism have taught me to ask questions, including What do I do about communion?

As a child growing up in Nashville, I didn't ponder this question. In my family, we lit the Sabbath candles, ate challah, and sipped grape juice from a sterling silver goblet, but no one identified the weekly ritual as the communion it really was. Though I have come to understand communion as a ritual intended to bring its participants into union with the divine, back then, I thought of it only in terms of the Eucharist. When our temple religious education class visited a Protestant or Catholic service, communion was a spectator sport.

It wasn't until I attended a three-day conference on ministry the summer prior to beginning divinity school that I came face to face with communion. During a workshop called "Holy Listening," the leader, a Methodist pastor, introduced the sacramental elements, pieces of muffin and orange juice, and invited each person to offer communion to the next person with the accompanying words, "I offer you the body and blood of Christ." I watched the tray of Dixie cups and the basket of muffins being passed around the circle and wondered what to do. Would it be rude to refuse or disingenuous to participate? Framing it as an expression of hospitality, I figured Jesus, who was at the center of the ritual, would be just fine with the lone Jew in a sea of Christians taking part.

Afterwards, concerned that I may have compromised the ritual for others by taking part, I said to the young man who had offered me the muffin bit and juice, "I hope it didn't offend you to offer a non-Christian communion," to which he replied, "It's not me I worry about; it's you."

His response intensified my quandary of what to do. Any other Jew I know would simply decline, and typically I do, but there are rare occasions when I feel called to do something else. For me, ritual, like language, forms a portal by which to access the divine or experience a fuller sense of union within it.

At my friend Calvin's ordination and again the first Sunday Calvin consecrated the Host and celebrated Eucharist, I was there to accept the "bread of heaven and the cup of life." It felt important and holy to receive the offering as a way of acknowledging not only Calvin's priesthood, but the priesthood of all believers, the concept that all are welcome and included at God's table. It brought me into deeper union with Jan Huss, the fourteenth-century Czech reformer who supported clergy who dared to offer the chalice to laity when that was considered a heretical act. And it invited me to consider how I might embody Jesus via his teachings.

I try to imagine what Jesus might have intended in the Jewish context of Passover as he offered his disciples wine and unleavened bread. I relate to the sacraments as symbols of his ministry—embodied in his willingness to place himself in peril in order to advance justice, mercy, and compassion.

Of Jesus's last Passover, Barbara Brown Taylor, an Episcopal priest and writer, asks,

> Why . . . did Jesus spend his last night on earth teaching
> his disciples to wash feet and share supper? With all the

conceptual truths of the universe at his disposal, he did not give them something to think about … instead he gave them concrete things to do—specific ways of being together in their bodies—that would go on teaching them what they needed to know. … [21]

Jesus's directive to taste the broken bread as his flesh—to know his body through the sacrament of shared food—emphasizes that words are metaphors for what the body knows. To know is to be embodied and embodiment is the source of knowing.

Framed this way, participating in communion does not feel like a betrayal of my Judaism, but rather a way to bridge a human-made divide. The Seder Jesus presided over in Jerusalem, like all Seders, would have centered around the commandment to commemorate the Exodus by experiencing it. So in that spirit, I come to the communion table or rail, not often and not as a Christian, but as a believer in the power of ritual to deepen connection.

The flower communion originated by the Czech Unitarian Norbert Capek celebrates the deep connection of human life to flower, the way sunlight and water nourish us, the way mortality intensifies the value of our days, the way each blossom and each person gives unique expression to shared qualities.

Communions of cornbread and challah embody sustenance and the hopefulness that rises in the human heart as surely as yeast leavens bread.

In Ontario, a congregant offered a strawberry communion in June when the local berries burst into full flavor. This Easter, I offer a chocolate communion where the sacrament represents life's sweetness and its trials, for in our Unitarian Universalist tradition, one does not emerge without the other.

Since toddlerhood, chocolate has been my favorite food.

---

21 Taylor, Barbara Brown, *An Altar in the World*, p. 43

Hardly a day goes by without me ingesting it. So imagine my horror many years ago when the cover of *Ms.* magazine proclaimed that chocolate was tainted by slavery. I don't know what allowed me to compartmentalize that information that almost all chocolate at that time involved exploited children trapped in horrendous working conditions, but somehow I kept eating chocolate.

Fortunately today we can buy fairly traded chocolate, but there remains rampant exploitation. Children are still trafficked, some kidnapped, others forced by parents to cross borders to work in the cacao groves. Children and adults exposed to hazardous pesticides and dangerous equipment toil with no safety checks in place. Their backbreaking labor yields most workers little recompense.

So often our sweetness is borne out of exploitation—but with mindfulness we can choose the fruits of justice and compassion. Today's sacramental chocolate is manufactured by an upscale chocolatier named Larry Burdick in Walpole, New Hampshire. The cacao comes from farmers in Grenada Burdick has partnered with to cultivate a just livelihood. The bittersweetness of the chocolate reminds us there is still justice to be done: workers waiting to be seated at the table of welcome.

Easter arises out of brokenness of body, and forms in the sweetness of redemption.

The chocolate has been chosen and broken with intention to invite us into deeper union with all that is holy: from the trees that bear the cacao pods to the splendor of our taste buds, to connection we share with all the beings involved in the fruition of chocolate.

As we take, taste, and savor, we sanctify plant matter and labor made holy by our gratitude, our remembrance, our yearning for justice, our embodiment of paradox and possibility. We redeem ourselves and our species when we choose mindfulness.

On many a Friday evening in childhood I experienced the recitation of the *Shema: Shema Israel, Adonai Eluhanu Adonai Ehud.*

Hear O Israel, The Lord Our God, The Lord is One.

The joined voices in temple taught me there are many ways to commune with the divine. Proclaiming God's Oneness and our place within it can happen with words or a wafer, matzoh or muffin, even chocolate. That we breathe and imagine, that we love and taste and fear is made possible by embodiment. Our senses inform our sensibilities. Our nerve endings and emotions allow us joy and suffering, and as such teach us compassion and seed in us the yearning for justice, mercy, and hope.

In the Christian tradition, communion is an invitation to experience Jesus's incarnation; here, communion invites us to experience our own.

Under the Tent

As a child raised in the South, I grew up steeped in the cadence of tent revivalists who preached with a fervor that electrified the air waves. Those Pentecostal voices entranced me, a Jewish kid who knew nothing of the theological underpinnings of either the Pentecost or the modern tradition borne in 1906 on Azusu Street. About a quarter of the world's Christians are Pentecostal, and while many of the other three-quarters blanch with embarrassment when their Pentecostal brethren speak in tongues or collapse from being overcome by the spirit, I am envious. I love such a visceral and audible expression of faith.

According to the *Anchor Bible Dictionary*, Pentecost is

> the Greek name for the Jewish Feast of Weeks, deriving from its occurrence 50 days after Passover. . . . According to [the book of] Acts, the apostles remained in Jerusalem after the Resurrection appearances. On the day of Pentecost they were gathered in one house when the Holy Spirit came upon them, sounding like a mighty wind and appearing like tongues of fire. . . . The apostles miraculously began to speak in foreign languages.

I can imagine *Ruach*, the Holy Wind, blowing through my window, rustling me in language trees would understand.

Pentecostal folk don't just think about God or discuss complex metaphysical concepts, they open themselves to a direct experience with the divine. Transcendentalists such as Emerson and Thoreau may be the closest religious liberals get to Pentecostal desire to feel the unmediated and unmitigated presence of holiness.

At Harvard Divinity School, where most worshipped at the altar of the intellect, a handful of African-American Pentecostal students gathered weekly for prayer. They stood in a circle and experienced God, felt God's presence embodied far deeper than words. They knew what I have come to realize: that all words are metaphors for what the body experiences.

God transforms from word to vibration to a palpable sensation. No wonder I loved the way certain phrases feel in my mouth. To say, "I'm feeling strong in the Lord this morning" becomes a portal that opens me to a spirit not confined or defined by words. The connotations evaporate and suddenly the purpose becomes evident: to make tangible what is usually beyond our grasp.

We don't always apprehend the holy so we create metaphors to ensnare it. Out beyond the edge of a revival tent are all the ones yearning to feel connection, to feel deeply beyond doubt a sense of belonging. The liberal Protestant theologian Sally McFague writes of the earth as the body of God. In the words of the great a cappella group Sweet Honey in the Rock, God embodied in Jesus becomes "My Rose of Sharon, sweet." Armenian Orthodox theologian Vigen Guroian speaks to the presence of God in the garden in his book *The Fragrance of God.*

> I'm walking in my garden and all of a sudden, overnight, something has bloomed, maybe the honeysuckle, maybe the rugosa roses, or maybe it's just the cabbage in the vegetable garden. And I don't even see it, but I know it's present. I feel its presence. No, I smell its presence. I'm aware of it. For many of us, that's an experience like that of experiencing God in prayer.
>
> . . .
>
> Much like the rose I sensed in the nursery, God is mysteriously present in our lives. Although I had forgotten the scent and the rose was out of view, its fragrance awakened me to its presence. We may not see God face to face or tangibly experience him in other ways, nonetheless, he avails himself to us as he did to Adam and Eve in the Garden.

Guroian maintains smell is the most mystical sense. It's also the sense most closely tied to memory. If a familiar smell can conjure an earlier experience, and in effect transport us to a different moment in time, can our notion of God or the holy as something containable, linear, reducible to simple description, collapse—and in its place emerge an opening to a world directly experienced, the Holy Wind blowing through us as if we were a screen? If we open the window could we feel what our Pentecostal brothers and sisters would recognize as the Holy Spirit?

There is wisdom to worshipping under a tent. It is open on all sides. In the book of Exodus, Moses pitched "the tent of meeting" wherein "the pillar of cloud would descend and stand at the entrance of the tent, and the Lord would speak with Moses" (Ex 33:7-10). Later, the tabernacle, the tent sanctuary, became "the central place of worship . . . a visible sign of Yahweh's presence. . . . More verses of the Pentateuch are devoted to it than any other object." Interestingly, the tabernacle contains not just the Ark of the Covenant but an incense altar, a seven-light candelabra, and Aaron's staff that miraculously blossomed.[22] Those early held objects to engage the senses.

In the book of Exodus, God appears in a burning bush and commands Moses to remove his sandals because he's standing on holy ground. God manifests in a way Moses can sensually apprehend. God instructs Moses to remove the leather from his feet so he can *feel* the ground of all being and physically experience its hallowedness. The essence of Pentecost is to feel the sacred, not simply to ponder its meaning.

Worshipping under a tent reminds us we are not impervious: to weather, to the unexpected, to mystery itself. Tents, like screens, permit direct connection. When the breeze blows we can feel it.

Tents are also portable. Nomads rely on them. Nowadays, as we spend much time encased in buildings and cars, nomads of a

---

22 *Anchor Bible Dictionary*, vol. 6

different sort, we cut ourselves off from what grounds us—from the very elements we yearn to experience. At best, most of us seek moderated interaction. No hurricanes, tsunamis, Santa Ana winds. We like calm skies, gentle breezes, surfable waves, though Moses would surely testify that no one can tell *Ruach* how or when to blow. In the original experience of Pentecost, God came in tongues of fire.

Holiness unbound. That is what lures me to Pentecostalism: that direct, uncontrolled, unmitigated experience with the holy ,however it manifests itself. The totality of experience that's also the root of wholeness.

To be filled, even overcome with spirit, is not a metaphor; it *is* the direct experience. It can knock us down, even flatten us; but it will not leave us unmoved. In our liberal religious, often cerebral, tradition, we gravitate to the spiritual equivalent to armchair travel, preferring the safety and tidiness of modulated words that suggest the feel of a place without actually traveling to it.

But just as a photo cannot capture the taste of a ripe strawberry or the scent of a tomato plucked fresh from the vine, words devoid of feeling, and life sanitized of grit, keep us from holiness unbound. The tent revivalists, ancient and contemporary, understand the way the Holy Spirit permeates all life.

Rumi, the thirteenth-century Sufi whose mystical poetry has brought many into communion with the divine, wrote:

> I am morning mist,
> And the breathing of evening.
> I am the wind in the top of a grove,
> and surf on the cliff....
> The musical air coming through a flute,
> a spark off a stone, a flickering in metal....
> Rose and nightingale
> lost in the fragrance.

The world beckons, its tent flaps blowing. Hallelujah and amen.

On Death and Being

Tomorrow is Memorial Day, a day we commemorate fallen soldiers, but approaching it more broadly, it's a day that invites us to remember the people whose imprint lingers. As we recall the people whose lives have touched ours in memorable ways, we conjure moments recent and long past, even fleeting, when a spark of kindness or decency charged us, when the gift of patience or compassion changed us, even now.

Often, we remember the people who had such an effect on our lives without knowing that we have done the same for someone else. At every memorial service I officiate I remind listeners the fullness of a life is not measured by longevity, but by the impressions made.

Considering the perennial question of what happens when we die, of course I have no answer but a thought has come to me I'd like to share. In the Jewish mystical tradition, a story of creation exists that goes something like this: When the divine energy needs to make room for the world it has to recede. A rabbi explained it to me this way: Visualize an inflated balloon deflating. Then somehow it bursts into infinite pieces. Sparks of divine light fall everywhere. The task of creation for humans is to recognize the divine light in each being, to gather it up, to reassemble its constituent parts. Perhaps each of us, not just the collective divine energy, eventually reassembles as a complete being.

I imagine Eeyore with his busted balloon gathering the pieces into a honey pot. If the purpose of life is to let ourselves be re-assembled or reunited with our own divine fragments as we lift up and return the divine fragments of others, then perhaps what happens in death is that, once again, the divine light within us scatters. It doesn't dissipate so much as disperse. Instead of residing in the body we once had, our light travels with any and every being we touched. The ones who love us. The ones who learn something about themselves by encountering us, even disliking us. The ones we inspire, mentor, raise. The ones we challenge in ways that evokes their growth, cultivates their flexibility, or patience, or understanding. The ones we extended our compassion to, and the ones who gained the capacity to be compassionate by knowing us.

Consider all the beings, not just people, who have touched, shaped, even defined your life, and consider as well your effect on others. Usually we don't have an accurate idea of the scope or depth of our influence. Perhaps that's why at calling hours and memorial services we recount the ways the deceased affected our lives. Imagine if you will all the fragments of our essential being: whether it be our sense of humor or our tenacity, our wisdom or our charm, our foibles, our resilience, our suffering, our joy, even our need—each carried in the vessel of someone else. It is not just a matter of being recalled. It's a matter of becoming part of what imprints another. We tread across sand and the grains shift all the way out to the ocean floor.

Perhaps in death our essential energy scatters the way light entering a prism refracts into multiple rainbows, which suggests the light we leave behind reflects the light we find, the light in others we lift up during our lives, however brief or long they may be.

If Memorial Day is a time to commemorate the dead it is also a time to consider the ways death doesn't end us. In her fanciful novel *A Gracious Plenty*, Sheri Reynolds writes:

> The dead coax the natural world along. . . . [They] control
> the seasons. . . . In June, the dead tunnel earthworms, crack
> the shells of bird eggs, poke the croaks from frogs. The ones

who died children make play of their work, blowing bugs
from weed to weed, aerating fields with their cartwheels....
The ones who died old cue the roosters to crow and dismiss
the dawn each morning.... The ones who died strong push
the rivers downstream. ... The ones who died shy string
spiderwebs, almost invisible. There's a job for everybody on
any given day. The Dead are generous with their gifts to the
living.

Not everyone perceives the dead this way, but as the protagonist
of the novel notes, she can see those who have died only by
remembering the shape they held in the past, "but that's about *my
eyes*—not [their] presence."[23]

Memorial Day creates an opening through which to return
our attention to the presence of those we carry with us, whether
they are dead or not. And it invites us to consider the ways we
inhabit not just the memory, but the sensibility of others.

So often we don't realize the effect we have on others, or
they on us. For eleven years I have carried a little boy named
John Gustin with me. I met John on the pediatric floor of Maine
Medical Center, where I did Clinical Pastoral Education, the
hospital chaplaincy program required for ministers in training.
John was seven the summer of 2000. From the notes in his chart I
knew he was nonverbal without any medical explanation noted;
that his mother was out of the picture; that his father and two
older brothers lived four hours away. Every day I would visit John,
grateful for the chance to hang out without having to worry about
words. There was no small talk to make. Just quiet playing and
the occasional words I offered him. He was quiet even beyond
his wordlessness, in his manner. He moved slowly, deliberately,
gently. He had been hospitalized because of an infection around
the insulin pump in his abdomen, but most days, he appeared
not to be in pain. John liked to play at the computer in the patient

---

23 Reynolds, Sheri, *A Gracious Plenty*

lounge and I will always remember the day I found him entranced by the figures on the screen. I asked if he would be willing to color with me for a while, being the low-tech person I am. I can still see him registering my request, considering his options to pass the time. In a moment, he lifted his index finger with its dirty little fingernail and pressed the off button. I have never felt so loved in all my life.

And because the universe is benevolent, one of my last days there, I happened on John in his room while a lovely pet therapy volunteer brought out an enormous white bunny. I sat down on John's bed and stroked the rabbit's soft fur with him when the volunteer offered to take our picture. I knew there would have been no way to photograph John myself as that would have been a violation of confidentiality and a breach of my role, but when the volunteer handed us each a Polaroid print I smiled and silently thanked the universe.

I treasured that photo because it allowed me to more readily revisit the time I spent with John, the way he instructed me in how to be present and attentive. He provided an easy way for a nervous novice to pass the days without having to knock on doors or enter rooms of other patients less eager to see a chaplain.

Over the years I have wondered what became of him. A few years ago I went on to Facebook thinking I might find him there, but I found only other folks with the same name. And for some inexplicable reason about a week and a half ago, I decided to try again. I went on to Facebook, typed in his name, and got a link to his obituary. John died six months after I last saw him, in the hospital at age eight.

I have been carrying his light, thoroughly illumined by the vision of that small finger pressing the computer button. I have held fast to the feeling of John one of the last times I encountered him, curled in my lap, his arms wound tightly around me, his head burrowed in my neck. I heard him crying and followed the sound into his room where a young nurse's aide brusquely combed his freshly shampooed hair. Suddenly, John began to wretch and the newly made bed was instantly soiled. Exasperated, the young aide yanked the sheets beneath him, so I carried John to the couch and cradled him. The trust he bestowed charged and changed me that August day, in a way that enlivens us both still.

When I speak of the universe holding us, this is what I mean. We are held in body, but also in memory. Whether we recognize it or not, we are held by those who carry us, and those we carry. We are held by the places we have trod, the trees trunks we leaned against. We are held in the stories others tell.

Sheri Reynolds writes in *A Gracious Plenty*, "I know the Dead haven't disappeared because the sun does rise. The roosters do crow. The clouds move across the sky like always."

After my father died in 1999, a year or two after I read Sheri's book, which, by the way, I bought seventeen copies of and gave out to friends, I began to think of my father pushing the tomato plants up each summer because of the way he devoured the box of Tennessee tomatoes his sister shipped him every year. He would sit down with a box of Saltines, a handful of red tomatoes, and a serrated knife and eat slices on crackers as if every one were his last and happiest meal.

Before my father left this life to ripen tomatoes, he married three times, first my mother, then his second and third wives. The last two left their marriage to him and got involved with a woman. During my father's cancer, when there was time to ruminate, we wondered aloud what were the odds of that. At the time my father met his second and third wives, they had been bobbing in rough seas—and I sense in him they found a safe harbor. My father was a gentle, supportive man. In his later marriages he had come to understand more of himself. From the pier where I stand looking back, I see how each woman gathered her strength and re-charted her course. And if someone were to say to me, "Gosh, your dad was married and divorced three times; too bad none of his marriages worked out," I would tell the story of his memorial service, where all three ex-wives gathered to hold him. I would speak of the Russian émigré who told the people gathered, all strangers to her, how my father had saved her life by helping her come to America. I would express how proud I am to be the daughter of a man who ushered women to safer shores.

Relationships serve a purpose beyond our line of sight. They don't have to last to work. I left Maine Medical Center eleven summers ago but I never set John B. Gustin II down.

Down a logging road where I walk my dog there's a pond where she likes to wade. Sometimes if I stand on a particular rock facing the pond when the sun is overhead, the light shimmers in waves up a tree at the water's edge. Streamers of fast-moving light skitter up and across the branches like a thousand tiny lizards racing to the top, never stopping. No doubt there's a scientific explanation, but I prefer to watch transfixed and thank "the dead [so] generous with their gifts to the living."

Come to the
Window

Holy Disruption

Years ago when I taught, just as some brilliant thought reached my lips, the campus belltower would invariably chime. Suddenly I was forced to decide: Should I plow onward, my cogent observation or tantalizing question too imperative to pause? Or should I wait patiently as the notes tarried, signaling the passing of yet another quarter hour? Faced with this perennial dilemma, I came upon a lovely meditation by Thich Nhat Hanh, suggesting that we let any sound of bells draw us into a moment of meditation regardless of where we are. When I announced this to a class of first-year university students, they groaned, no doubt considering the invitation into compassion for their fellow beings a bit much in the middle of a required composition course. So even if I lacked the wherewithal to overtly observe that moment of meditation or insist that my students do the same, inwardly, I ceased thinking of the chimes as an intrusion, or at least an unwelcome one.

As a minister this has helped. In my previous life as a congregant, I found the cries of babies disruptive, the inevitable coughs and sneezes during the prayerful silences a bit disconcerting, and the stirrings of my fellow worshippers distracting. The mindfulness of Thich Nhat Hanh rescued me from myself and allowed me to hear the audible signs of life around me as a song of connection, ever reminding me that I am part of a great cosmos pulsing with activity. Thankfully, I have gained more than tolerance. I have come to appreciate ringing bells and cell phones, sneezes and coughs, whispers and cries as a banner of sound heralding life on life's terms, summoning all of us to leave the private zone of our own momentary existence to join the whole of life in its whirring and whooshing across the threshold.

During a service that fell on the extra day of a Leap Year, in the midst of a reading, a ringing sounded. I made a lighthearted comment and moved on. Admittedly, I thought little of the circumstances behind the noise. A mobile phone or pager. A busy life. Nothing more.

Now that cell phones populate the landscape, most of us are inured or simply relieved when ours doesn't ring at an inopportune time. After the service, a congregant approached me to apologize. He explained he delivered time-sensitive medical equipment: computer systems and neonatal units, and sometimes organs or blood.

On February twenty-ninth, a day that rolls around once every four years, someone on the other end of theinterruption awaited a human heart. A heart bound for transport, a heart just extracted from a body that moments before still contained the breath of life. A life interrupted far more aggressively than with the ringing of bells.

That's the reality of heart transplants. Someone has to die abruptly in order to harvest a healthy heart. There can be no extraordinary life-saving measures, no iced organ rushed in a cooler to an airstrip, no prayers answered by successful surgery, no family weeping with relief *unless* another family gathers elsewhere to grieve the shards of a shattered life.

The poet and essayist Wendell Berry writes, "We live the given life, and not the planned."

We who enjoy the great freedom and luxury to gather in worship each Sunday, to enjoy quietude, to live lives that are rarely punctuated by the sound of alarms, all know the sound of sirens. If we are lucky, the stories behind the sirens do not belong to us, at least not intimately, but for some of us, they do.

Sirens scream for a reason. Not just to get our attention in traffic—summoning us to pull over so an emergency vehicle can pass. They scream for the same reason we do: to express urgency, call for help, and holler, "Hey, everything is not going according to plan." Interruptions defy our desires, even our will. Some bring about the end of a life. And sometimes, that end is not a wall but a wire connecting itself to a life in a distant city. It runs through a pager in a pocket, through the man who must decide whether to answer the call, to leave worship, to leave his children off somewhere so he can transport a heart. It runs through him and all of us who know nothing of the story but are touched in this way by it still, to the person waiting for a second chance, a medical intervention intended to prolong a life, perhaps in some deeper sense, two.

Rebecca Parker, president of the Starr-King School for the Ministry, one of two Unitarian Universalist seminaries, speaks of holy disturbances, disruptions that call us to higher ground. Moments ripe for transformation. In the *Book of Runes*, a Viking oracle enjoying widespread use today, Ralph Blum echoes this concept in his description of the rune or pictograph *Hagalaz* as a rune of elemental disruption, events totally beyond our control, [heralding a disruption in plans] so great as to tear fabric of one's reality, security and self-understanding. Ralph Blum writes that even though "you may sustain loss or damage—a tree falls on your home, a relationship fails, plans go wrong, a source of supply dries up . . . you are not without power in the situation. The inner strength you have funded until now in your life is your support and guide." If one consults the oracle of runes and draws *Hagalaz*, one is "forewarned and therefore, encouraged to understand . . . the radical discontinuity" as "necessary for growth." When one encounters this rune, it "indicates a pressing need within the psyche to break free from constricting identification with material reality."

I have experienced the power of holy disturbance, *Hagalaz*. I have upended my own plans, interrupted my own narrative, disrupted the very reality, security, and self-understanding Blum writes about. Not consciously. Not intentionally. The psyche has a way of breaking free, of releasing us from whatever threatens our most honest growth. When our egos get in the way by creating some plan, erecting some blueprint of how we should be, or the strictures of familial, social, or professional pressure confine us in unhealthy ways, the psyche engineers disruption. A disturbance made holy by its desire to set us free.

In her book *She's Not There*, Jennifer Finney Boylan chronicles "a life in two genders," documenting forty years of life lived as a male and experienced as female. Boylan's earliest awareness during boyhood of an inexplicable feeling of femaleness sets up an internal struggle for truth. As a young man Boylan longs to be "cured by love." When he goes in search for answers from a gender specialist who identifies him as a transsexual, he says, "I wanted to learn how to accept who I wasn't. What I felt was, being a man might be the second best life I can live, but the *best* life I can live will mean only loss and grief. So what I wanted to learn was how to be happy with this second life."

And indeed, Boylan tries. As James he marries and fathers two children. He publishes books and climbs the academic ladder. And after a number of years, the psyche, apparently discontent to stay locked in the basement any longer, disrupts Boylan's life. He returns to therapy. He tells his wife he can't go on living as a man.

Imagine if you will your partner, your parent, your child telling you that she or he can no longer continue living with the gender the world assumes. The HBO film *Normal* with Jessica Lange and Tom Wilkinson renders such a drama. Both the movie and Boylan's book make clear the disruption. And while one may understand how the psyche of a transgender person forces an interruption so that the true gender of the person can emerge, what about the overturned life of the spouse whose "reality, security, and self-understanding" shatter in the storm of *Hagalaz*?

Grace Finney Boylan tells her husband, "I want what I had."

"We live the given life, not the planned."

A siren wails and lives unravel.

A body lies in an autopsy room. A family shudders with unexpected loss.

A pager beeps in a sanctuary. A heart awaits transport.

A family gathers around a hospital bed, hands clenched, hoping. A surgical team prepares.

On Boylan's birthday, after seeing the endocrinologist who prescribes female hormones, Grace gives her spouse a card that reads, "Here's to forty-two years of joy and struggle, conflict and resolution, dreams and possibilities. And with love for all that's yet to come." Sitting at the edge of the water with Grace, Boylan, now known as Jenny, swallows her first Premarin tablet with a mouthful of champagne.

Grace Finney Boylan does not get back what she had. Nor does Jessica Lange's character, Irma, in the movie *Normal*. Both women get something else, a life far different and more complex than either would have imagined. Perhaps a life blessed in ways neither could foresee. Neither can control what happens yet both get to choose how they respond, and in that essential way, they determine what their lives become.

Like so many of us, they face the unimagined. I think of my brother's unexpected death at eighteen. I think of a schoolmate who went out west at nineteen only to be brought home two weeks later after a psychotic break that evidenced paranoid schizophrenia. I think of family friends whose fourth child was born with a defective heart. There are countless ways life interrupts our plans. Falling in or out of love at inopportune moments. Losing a job, suffering ill health, having an accident. Boarding a plane bound for Los Angeles on a day terror takes to the skies.

We all suffer in life. In large ways or small. We all face the unexpected because none of us know what awaits us. There is nothing ennobling about suffering disruption, but the choice we have in our response is what Victor Frankl calls the last of human freedoms. We can choose to step into the great unknown, to weather the hurricane that someone else's psyche brings about. We can batten down the hatches and grieve as disruption levels our dreams and then walk through the wreckage to salvage and find anew building blocks of reconstruction.

Somewhere a pager beeps, a cell phone rings, a siren wails. The sounds that interrupt connect us. Listen to bells ringing. Attend to stirring storms. Survey the debris with openness. Life calls to us. Possibility resonates within each sound.

To Be of Use

The work of the world is unevenly shared; still it belongs to us all. Whether we meet that work as burden or privilege, obligation or invitation determines whether we will sing in the traces.

A young nurse's aide enters a hospital room to find a woman sore, fatigued, and bandaged from surgery, staring at her dinner tray unable to get the food to her mouth. The nurse's aide is there to record the patient's vital signs. She has many rooms to get to before her shift ends but instead of scurrying out, she sits down to feed the woman staring helplessly at her food. It isn't in the young woman's job description. Or is it? What are we called to do?

If, as Marian Wright Edelman says, "service is the rent we pay for being; it is the very purpose of life, not something we do in our spare time," the young woman does what is hers to do. Her actions may seem remarkable in a world where service gets confused with servitude. In our fast-paced, technological, high-efficiency culture where profit functions as the dominant value, the idea of work for work's sake, or service as spiritual rent, becomes an anomaly. It's one thing to work to pay the rent or mortgage, to feed the family, or afford a nice vacation, but in a secular world, the sound of voices rising from the traces gets lost amid the whirr of increased productivity and the din of exploitation.

In religious communities of all kinds, service takes on a very different meaning. In the words of Joan Chittister, a Benedictine nun and prolific writer, "Work is co-creative. We work because the world is unfinished and it is ours to develop. Work is not a private enterprise. Work is not to enable [us] to get ahead; the purpose of work is to enable [us] to get more human and make [our] world more just."

If "service is the rent we pay for being," it begs the question:

Who is the landlord? For Joan Chittister and many of our co-religionists, "Work is a commitment to God's service." God puts the *lord* in landlord. But for those who may not find God a useful concept, to whom or what do we pay spiritual rent? We pay it to each other, we pay it to the cosmos, which brings us forth out of the stardust; we pay it to trees and plants and waterways that enable our survival. We pay it to the animals and ecosystems that sustain us.

It is not just Benedictine spirituality that reminds us service is to be done for its own sake, "that work develops the worker." Think of the nurse's aide in the hospital room. It may have been her job to take a blood pressure reading or jot some notation in the chart. But what more glorious task is there than to feed another being, to participate in the sustenance of life?

Ironically, the patient had been a hospital dietician who taught all the food service workers she supervised that their work was the most important. Without food, the patients would perish and there would be no need for doctors, nurses, and scientific research.

Admittedly, in a status-driven culture, we might overlook people who perform what we consider menial tasks. In her poem, "Singapore," Mary Oliver encounters a woman in the airport washing the tops of ashtrays in a toilet bowl. At first, the poet feels disgust; but as she observes the woman working she sees beauty as she recognizes the light emanating from the woman's life. When we sing in the traces, the light shines.

Probably most of us here have labored in traces of one sort or another: in fields or factories, along roadsides or grounds. I recall visiting a friend in prison who had been working in the bakery, enjoying, in prison terms, favorable working conditions and a good rate of pay—until a correctional officer with a bad attitude fired him. For a while he got assigned "yard duty," scooping goose poop and picking up trash. At first he resented it but then he told me, "Maybe I needed it. I was getting a little cocky. It's not so bad walking the grounds, making the place look nicer." He reminded me of the three weeks I spent one summer cleaning washrooms at a public beach. Though unpleasant, it gave me time to consider all the occasions I've stepped into a public washroom and been delighted to find it clean.

Consider all the work easily overlooked that makes a difference. Simple acts of courtesy or kindness, patience or humor. The bathroom attendant who smiles and means it. The server who accommodates a special meal. The nurse's aide who feeds a hungry patient. The clerk who sorts out a complicated return. The chef who rolls up his sleeves and helps with the dishes. The physician who pulls up a chair and sits with a frightened patient for a while. Workers in every echelon who recognize service as its own reward.

To be of use without thought of recompense or accolade is the work of co-creation.

Service is not about servitude. To serve creation is to complete it. The great evolutionary chain of being that gathers periodic elements and fashions them into stars that explode and humans who compose requires participation. Look at ants and bees: their elaborate social structures that serve creation, not just themselves. The natural world abounds with examples of inter-species interaction and reliance. The universe is designed to bring us into relationship, engaging us in the acts of co-creation all the time. No one gets a free pass.

Work must honor the ones who labor. The sixth-century Rule of Benedict instructed its monastic followers to assist workers: to provide adequate food and rest, to amend the task if it is too taxing. In an era when slavery commonly existed, the followers of St. Benedict understood the spiritual imperative not to live off the labor of others or consider oneself part of an elite class. In our industrialized, globalized capitalistic society, we depend on the labor of others, mostly the labor of those we will never meet.

If we believe their work serves the greater community, the

community we create must serve justice. To ask others to toil as we ourselves would not do is fundamentally unjust. While we each have certain abilities and skills that help us divide the work of a given community, we endanger ourselves if we succumb to divisions based on caste or class. If we remove ourselves from the work of the world we forget our rightful place in the scheme of creation.

And if we neglect to service ourselves in the ways that allow us to be of service to others, we undermine justice and respect. Just as our Unitarian Universalist principles call on us to respect the worth of all and to uphold human rights and meet basic human needs, we must tend to our own gardens. If we fail to take rest, to engage in holy leisure, to care for our own well-being, we reduce our capacity to be of service and to take joy in it. Without the joy, without singing in the traces, work becomes drudgery, not service. It depletes. Thus, service encompasses not only the giving *of* self, but giving *to* ourselves.

Unfortunately, the term "self-serving" carries negative connotations—a form of selfishness—whereas "self-service" often indicates an invitation to be self-sufficient or independent. But in truth, such independence is an illusion. When we pull up to the self-serve gas pump and pump it ourselves, we rely on legions of workers from the oil fields and refineries to transport drivers to the farmers who grow the food to feed those workers and the garment makers who produce their uniforms and the people who harvest the rubber for the truck tires and road crews who pave the roads, and the dentists who keep the truck drivers and oil workers from missing work due to painful rotting teeth, to say nothing of all the plants, minerals, and animals involved. All of us rely on the efforts of countless other beings *and* our own efforts. Part of our responsibility as earthly servants is to maintain ourselves. We maintain our automobiles and our buildings, our equipment and our tools, so why not maintain ourselves? And one of the ways we can do that is by recognizing the value of service for its own sake.

Think of how stressed any of us can become when we feel we are wasting time, not doing the "real" work, the important stuff. What are we doing rinsing the cups in the sink when we could be finding a cure for cancer or raising money to fight poverty? Why make phone calls to rustle up volunteers for a church committee when we could design a building or wire a house?

The summer I did hospital chaplaincy, I spent Wednesdays at an outpatient cancer clinic. I just roamed the room chatting with people as their chemo dripped. It was easy to see the hours spent as unimportant, not particularly useful to anyone, except of course the experience taught me a great deal about courage and humility, tenacity and faith. But at the end of the summer as I bid goodbye to a man I had frequently enjoyed talking with, he looked me in the eye and thanked me. He told me that my presence had made the experience easier. And even though I didn't know why, I believed him. I was given the privilege to be of service in ways I could not fully understand. I had no idea that June day I first arrived that sixteen months later I would conduct Wayne's memorial service, because in his mind, I had become his pastor. I had no way of knowing as I sat talking with Wayne about fishing or woodworking, that after he died, his stepdaughter would ask me to officiate at her wedding. To be of use, to be invited to serve the ever-unfolding process of creation.

We don't know in each moment the fullness of our service. We don't often comprehend the entirety of its meaning, to ourselves or to each other. Just when we think humans are rotten, a nurse's aide pulls up a chair and gently feeds the patient who cannot lift her own fork. Such a simple gesture not only nourishes the body, it restores faith in the kindness of strangers. A man stoops to scoop goose poop in a prison yard, making the green space beneath razor wire feel more welcoming. Everyday common acts affirm inherent worth and dignity.

The traces stretch out before us: there's much work to do.

Nothing builds community more than the combined efforts of us all. Many hands make fulfilling work; and in every act of service, no matter how menial or mundane, we regenerate the beauty of Creation. Across the fields a song rises, inviting us to harmonize, to join in the work that binds us and allows us to rise up singing.

Cultivating Faith

I've been thinking a lot about faith lately. The sweeping narrative of Passover, the faith of the Israelites who fled Egypt to wander for forty years, unsure where they would end up or what would be asked of them. Easter, of course, with its central story of resurrection. The snowdrops and tendrils of green pushing up through the mud tell their own faith story this time of year. It is a season of faith.

There is a children's story about faith I love to tell from a book called *Wanda's Roses*[24] where a girl about nine passes by a vacant lot filled with trash on her way to school. Wanda notices a scraggly thornbush amid the garbage and, certain it is a rosebush, she lovingly tends it. As she drags old tires and garbage away, the adults in the neighborhood try to tell her it's no rosebush, but Wanda persists. She asks the shopkeeper across the street for water; she enlists the school librarian in the care of roses. While the adults are busy trying to convince Wanda the thornbush will bear no roses, she tells them by summer the lot will be filled with their sweet scent. After weeks with no sign of a bloom, Wanda decides she is meant to bring roses to the bush so she spends an evening making paper blossoms to affix to the scraggly little plant. She invites the neighborhood adults to tea in her garden and they all come bearing rose bushes to plant so that by the time summer arrives, the lot indeed abounds with roses, just like Wanda said.

For some, faith conjures church services peppered with *amen*s and hands raised in praise; for me, it conjures Wanda and her roses. Faith is one of those words, like love, that gets tossed around and, in liberal religious circles, dismissed. Too often, the word gets

24 By Pat Brisson and Maryann Cocca-Leffler, published by Boyds Mills Press, 2000

associated with or co-opted by religious orthodoxies of all stripes that misconstrue it as something doctrinal or supernatural, when in reality, it needn't be either. Nora Gallagher, an astute Episcopal observer, writes, "Faith is not about belief in something irrational or about a blind connection to something unreal. It's about a gathering, an accumulation of events and experiences of a different order." Thus, faith is about a transforming reality and our capacity to be transformed by experiences of everyday life.

So what does that mean exactly? To be transformed by experiences of everyday life?

I suspect we have all felt transformed at one time or another: changed by someone's kindness or unconditional love. Transformed by witnessing extraordinary courage or graciousness. Changed by radical acceptance. For me, transformation comes when I accept the circumstances that befall and befuddle me. The times in my life when the heft of unfairness shifts because I realize the situation and the people I perceive as unfair are in fact my great teachers.

When I can set down the viewfinder of unfairness and pick up the monocle of faith, I see differently. I stop focusing on what aggrieves me and start seeing how I can be transformed by what's happening, whether I like it or not. For me, faith is neither hocus-pocus nor a suspension of disbelief. Rather it is simply the sum of evidence my life presents in unyielding measure of grace and growth amidst anguish and anxiety, bafflement, even despair.

Faith is not easy. All the more reason to heed the words of W. H. Auden, "to choose what is difficult all one's days as if it were easy." To choose what is difficult as if it were easy, not just once, but time and time again. To clear vacant lots mounded with rubbish day after day, wielding rake and trowel. To tend the neglected as graciously as the manicured. Daily, finding the garden in an abandoned plot.

Rosemary Bray McNatt, a Unitarian Universalist minister in New York City writes that "there are no grand gestures inherent in the day to day tedium of doing what you think is right." She recounts her experience of driving through the Lincoln Tunnel, where she passes a man asking for spare change. At first, she keeps her window rolled up, trying to second-guess what he'd do with the money. Eventually though, she decides to roll down her window, offer the man some change, bid him a pleasant day and encourage him to eat.

"I know when I do that," she writes, "I am trying to live faithfully. I am trying to affirm the inherent worth and dignity of every person. I am trying to adhere to the Buddhist principle of right conduct. I'm trying to recall the Biblical admonition to feed the hungry and the directive of Jesus to love your neighbor as yourself."

Living faithfully is no easy task. Whether in a nation rife with people who live on the street or in a country where the neglected reside primarily behind bars, tending to the abandoned with an open and loving heart means taking the road less traveled, reordering our priorities, and relinquishing the security of long-held beliefs.

For the German theologian Dietrich Bonhoeffer, choosing what was difficult meant leaving the safety of a teaching position in New York during World War II to return to home. In 1939 Bonhoeffer wrote, "I have come to the conclusion that I have made a mistake in coming to America. I must live through this difficult period . . . with the Christian people of Germany. I have no right to participate in the reconstruction of Christian life in Germany after the war if I do not share in the trials of this time with my people."

Bonhoeffer cast his lot with countrymen he could not abandon: an act of bravery that cost him his life. Arrested and imprisoned in 1943, he was hanged in 1945. Few of us face such dire circumstances, such painful decisions, but daily, we must face what is difficult and choose what we will do. Faith casts our lot not with what is possible, but what is right.

I think of the men and women I've met in prisons, the ones who choose each day to remake themselves, to accept sentences they cannot change in order to transform the time they must spend behind bars. I think of one man I befriended while he was in jail awaiting a federal sentence. He had already spent ten years in prison plagued with mental illness, praying fervently for help. When he got out, he tried to stay away from drugs and the chaos of addiction that had landed him behind bars. He began to turn his life around, until he got involved with a young woman addicted to crack.

I first listened to his story full of heartbreak and poor choices, good intentions and bad endings when I volunteered as a jail chaplain several years ago. Back then, he professed his faith and asked me to profess mine. For him, it was a simple formula: he recited a creed. But as the months dragged on while he awaited sentencing, keeping the faith took on a new dimension. He bargained with God. He erupted often in anger. Some days when I visited, he felt forsaken by a God he so desperately wanted to love. He came to understand that faith isn't as simple as "belief in something irrational or . . . a blind connection to something unreal."

Faith emerges when we look honestly at our own actions, when we embrace truths however painful they may be, and recognize that the things we run from *are* what lead us to the present moment. I suspect for many of us it's a lot easier to espouse faith than to keep it.

The stories I've heard, the truths I've encountered as a jail chaplain, as a prison volunteer, challenge my faith. The very same folks who insist this nation uphold a Judeo-Christian sensibility are often the folks insisting politicians are tough on crime without regard to prevention, treatment, or rehabilitation. I want to believe that all of us will somehow make better choices, that all of us will turn away from violence and toward a transforming power fueled by the recognition of each person's dignity and worth. But in the midst of harsh realities wrought out of fear and limitations, politics and human frailty, the only faith I can hold on to is the choice to do what is right—to spend the occasional weekend helping facilitate a prison workshop on Alternatives to Violence as an affirmation of my own faith that transformation *is* possible. I write letters to a young friend, recently sentenced to eight years in prison. I try to be present in the uncertainty, choosing to believe the words of Julian of Norwich: All shall be well.

We all know there are so many lives that resemble vacant lots. Lives full of brambles, dirty needles, beer bottles, and far too few roses. There isn't a rake or trowel big enough to plant a garden where every prison stands, where every woman forced into prostitution walks. But any of us, by choosing what is difficult as if it were easy, can tend seeds of compassion. When we practice acceptance and radical trust amid the most inhospitable conditions, we cultivate faith.

If we gather the transformative moments in our lives and extract their essence, we can experience the fragrance of possibility even before the bud opens and long after bloom disappears.

I'm the first to admit, it is much easier to talk about faith than to feel it. All of us have our own abandoned lots and some days, the challenge of choosing what is difficult means handing someone else the hoe or watering can. The accumulation of experience instructs us that tending the soul's garden is not something we can do alone. The little girl in the story who wants roses, the man in a New York tunnel asking for change, the minister who rolls down her window, Dietrich Bonhoeffer returning to Germany, my friend in his cell, and all the rest of us wherever we are, are in this together, part of the wholeness and inescapable interconnectedness of life.

That for me is where faith lies, in the connections that continue to surprise and sustain me. In those moments when I am bobbing to and fro and someone calls and I realize the power of connection can transform a vacant lot into a garden. Faith dwells too in the indomitable nature of the human spirit, the way people in horrible circumstances can still radiate light, the way pain, even suffering, can open petal by petal into a fragrant bloom.

In a troubled and troubling world, keeping the faith means choosing to rise above the weight of facts, the violent reiterations of human history that indicate we're doomed to repeat ourselves. Faith does not insist we deny the truth; rather it births in us larger possibilities, allowing us moments of grace the way dreams let us recognize languages we've never spoken or places we've never been.

Faith makes no promises other than the promise of grace— those moments amid the clanging bars and abandoned lots when the benevolence of the universe blossoms in a simple connection of care. A few years ago, I might have known in my head but not my gut how it feels to maintain faith without necessarily abating doubt.

But like Wanda in the story whose own doubt leads her not to give up but to make paper roses and organize a tea party instead, each of us has a choice every day to notice a barren thornbush and imagine the possibilities within.

In a world where war looms ever-present on the horizon and preventable suffering is infrequently stopped, it is far easier to lose faith than to keep it. To resist looking in dark corners for evidence of light. It's far more tempting to choose what is easy— to travel the road of complacency or tend only to patches of self-centeredness. That's why it's so important that we come together to reinforce and collaborate in simple acts of bravery—bearing witness, seeding compassion, telling the truth. If we can feel in our bodies sunlight and plant matter, our animal nature and human spirit, water and stardust, we will know what it means to be whole, to feel the stores of possibility in every cell. And that feeling allows us to embody faith —not just to imagine it but to keep it.

Look into someone's eyes.
Notice the world in your palm.
Accumulate experiences of a different order.
Choose what is difficult as if it were easy. Every day.
Carry tissue paper for roses.
Tend an abandoned lot.

We needn't immerse ourselves in a baptismal pool to demonstrate our faith. We needn't wave our arms or fall to our knees, though such responses might help reacquaint us with sky and earth. We need only carry a trowel.

With New Eyes and Ears

I am struck by the news coverage of the so-called "Jeremiah Wright controversy," how worshipful words taken out of context become not just incendiary but grossly misunderstood. What I cherish about Unitarian Universalism is our appreciation of multiple perspectives that afford us the eyes and ears to fully perceive context. Take, for example, a prayer not known to incite that we rarely recite in our sanctuaries, though many of us have some experience with it. The Lord's Prayer may sound benign to the casual listener but there is far more to it than initially meets the ear and eye.

Growing up in a Reform Jewish home, I did not encounter the Lord's Prayer other than the visit to a friend's church. It wasn't until a trip to Cuernavaca, Mexico, at a retreat center run by Benedictine nuns, that the Lord's Prayer took on new meaning. The sisters led worship four times a day. By the third day, I felt great spiritual loneliness. I'm not much of a singer and Benedictines sing most of the service, and the Trinitarian language felt so foreign, in Spanish or English. On my last day there, five of us met for midday worship—four nuns and me. The other American guests must have been packing. It was a brief service with a couple of songs and a gospel reading in Spanish. To close, the sisters stood in a circle beckoning me to join them, and in English, they recited the Lord's Prayer.

It was clearly their gift to me. They were not fluent, or even conversant in English, yet they gave of themselves what they had, and I took from that experience a new appreciation for the way prayer embodied the spiritual generosity of the nuns. But it wasn't until a course in divinity school, when we read *Jesus Before God: The Prayer Life of the Historical Jesus*, that I understood the Lord's Prayer in a completely different light as a prayer not so much of God but in the tradition of the Hebrew prophets.

The author of *Jesus Before God*, Hal Taussig, a scholar and pastor, maintains that a "group of Galilean sages living a generation after Jesus, managed almost by accident to preserve very valuable prayer material related to the historical Jesus."[25] Taussig claims this group, who, scholars now refer to as the Q movement, "began to institutionalize prayer as a response to their situation." As they critiqued the religious traditions of the synagogue, they encountered much resistance. The prayer they composed "claimed their connection to Jesus," and according to Taussig, it is far more likely to be a "Jewish prayer" that expresses the "embattled self-consciousness of the group under fire" that reminded them of Jesus, their spiritual founder, than words specifically uttered or taught by Jesus as the Gospels claim.

Taussig presents five variations on what he calls "Jesus prayers," all of which resemble and contain language recognizable in what we commonly refer to as "The Lord's Prayer."

The earliest version:

> Abba/Father,
> Your name be revered.
> Let your basilica/kingdom/reign come.
> Give us the bread we need for today
> And forgive us our debts to the extent we forgive those
> who are in debt to us.
> And please don't subject us to test after test.

Taussig provides historical context for each line, which expands the meaning exponentially, especially for Unitarian Universalists.

Take the first line: Taussig writes, "Seeing God as 'Abba/Father' was a clever combination of challenge to family tradition and evocation of a new trust in the divine fabric of life itself. Calling

---

25 Hal Taussig, *Jesus Before God: The Prayer Life of the Historical Jesus*

out to God as 'Abba/Father' replaced one's reliance on the family systems of privilege . . . and expressed Jesus' dependence on God alone."

Your name be revered or *hallowed be thy name* "belongs to a number of traditional prayers that almost every Jew in Galilee said regularly,"[26] but as Hal Taussig points out, there's a joke embedded in the line when combined with Abba/Father. Jews, both ancient and modern, especially the more orthodox among us today, utter only a transliteration of God's holy name. When first-century Jews revered the name of God, they thought of the name represented by the Hebrew consonants, YHWH, which we commonly pronounce as Yahweh. Thus, to revere God's name in the context of "Father" "called upon people to put God and reverence in a much broader perspective. (Taussig).

For Jesus, or the next generation or two of his followers, living under Roman rule, to pray for God's reign, on earth contained political overtones; God's reign in contrast to the Roman Empire, involved economic justice, power arising out of humility not force, radical hospitality, and a dismantling of oppression—in short, a new social order.

Give us the bread we need for today. Not enough for the week or the month or the year. Not a request that all our needs be met in this moment. Not plenty, not an excess. Simply a request for today's sustenance. The line becomes a call to mindfulness, to stay in the present moment—not to hoard or fret, but to live faithfully in the now. While it's prudent to plan for the future, put money into retirement, the line reminds us most of the world's people haven't the luxury to plan beyond the day. Reciting this line and the next becomes an act of solidarity if nothing else. Indebtedness, a major problem for the first-century followers of Jesus, remains a huge concern for many today. With the mortgage crisis, global food shortages, and soaring fuel costs, the historical context becomes ours.

---

26 Hal Taussig, *Jesus Before God: The Prayer Life of the Historical Jesus*

Forgive us our debts to the extent we forgive those who are in debt to us. The line as originally written addressed a pressing socio-economic issue. As the prayer changed, the focus broadened to address forgiveness in general, and reciprocity. As America's debt and that of its citizens mounts—economically and spiritually, what will happen if we are forgiven to the extent we are willing to forgive? Will our need for forgiveness entice us to forgive more? As our national debt ceiling grows, will we regard the debts of others with more compassion? One can only hope.

Hal Taussig writes,

> What is striking about the prayer . . . is how it demands engagement in social situations of the ones who are praying. . . . This kind of praying does not involve projecting one's voice to heaven. It does not require escaping into an interior realm. It meets God in the situation itself....God is the dynamic which connects everything in this kind of prayer. . . . God is that which connects everything on earth.

When I told my mother, who is here today, about this sermon, she said, "You're not going to be political, are you? You don't want to jeopardize their 501c3 status."

"No," I assured her, "it's not the role of the pastor or the congregation to be political; but it is our role to be prophetic."

And that got me thinking, with all the recent talk about the Rev. Jeremiah Wright, how context and connection *are* everything. I have heard Jeremiah Wright twice: in 1999 when he preached and gave a lengthy address at a conference on ministry, and in 2007, when he presented a three-hour program at the annual meeting of Unitarian Universalist ministers prior to our General Assembly. On both occasions, the Rev. Wright spoke eloquently and so knowledgeably about African-American church traditions, linguistics, music, history, and the importance of pastoring courageously, especially in communities where few if any are willing to speak truth to power, and where the powerful rarely listen.

He said nothing incendiary, and listening to his interview with Bill Moyers, I felt saddened Barack Obama has distanced himself so thoroughly, and sadder still that so many Americans—ignoring context and connection—are so quick to dismiss or demonize what Wright has to say. In his interview with Bill Moyers, he quoted a mentor of his, Martin Marty, who said what happens in church on Sunday has to relate to life in the world on Monday. And it's the prophetic tradition that connects the two. Sunday service is about more than offering comfort and shoring up hope—though those are important. It is a time to listen deeply and reflect on hard questions and demanding truths.

Wright also spoke of the sudden unpopularity of Martin Luther King, Jr. once he began speaking publicly against the war in Vietnam. While the Rev. Wright gains notoriety for sound bites lifted out of context, King is largely remembered in sound bites utterly removed from his adamant opposition to the war long before other public figures denounced it.

It's far more comfortable to recall King's exquisite metaphors, poetic language, and brilliant cadence than to heed his call to speak up and out, especially at great personal peril.

In rudimentary form, the phrases that became the Lord's Prayer were as unsettling to first-century listeners as King's anti-war speeches in the mid-1960s and the snippets of Jeremiah Wright's sermons to voters today. What all three texts have in common is a prophetic tradition of speaking truth to power, of daring to say what is unpopular, what challenges the comfort and complacency of listeners, especially those with privilege and power—such as ourselves.

Historically, Unitarianism and Universalism sprang directly from critical thought, from courageous men and women (though the men are the ones whose words got recorded) who dared to read the Bible and name the inconsistencies between scripture and church doctrine, who insisted upon religious tolerance and articulated a more compassionate understanding of God's love. Many were martyred for their interpretation and belief. And none of us would be sitting here in this service, in this sanctuary, without their willingness to speak their truth to those in power.

We, who have the luxury to assemble freely, to worship as we choose, bear the awesome responsibility to carry on that prophetic tradition. It is our legacy, no less than the Hebrew people freed by Moses so they enter into a covenant with God. We have been liberated and given a free church not to sit comfortably in our pews but to reckon with our role in righting wrongs.

Contained in the Hebrew Scriptures are the writings of twenty-one prophets. Among the most well known: Jeremiah, Isaiah, Hosea, Micah, and Amos. Prophets who often spoke on behalf of God, certain that they had been called upon to give human voice to divine disappointment. Prophets whose daring informed the sensibilities of our liberal religious forebears. Prophets who did not shirk their duty to express dire truths: to say, "things are terribly out of whack."

Listen to the prophet Ezekiel to whom the word of the Lord came:

> "In the abundance of your trade you were filled with violence, and you sinned." (28:16)

And to Jeremiah:

> "How can you say, 'We are wise and the law of the LORD is with us,' when in fact, the false pen of the scribes has made it into a lie?" (8:8) "[The wise] have treated the wound of my people carelessly, saying, 'Peace, peace.' When there is no peace. They have acted shamefully, they committed abomination; yet they were not at all ashamed, they did not know how to blush. Therefore they shall fall among those who fall; at the time when I punish them, they shall be overthrown, says the LORD." (8:11-12.)

And to today's Jeremiah:

> ... if you look at Deuteronomy, it talks about blessings and curses, how God doesn't bless everything. God does not bless gang-bangers. God does not bless dope dealers. God does not bless young thugs that hit old women upside the head and snatch their purse. God does not bless that. God does not bless the killing of babies. God does not bless the killing of enemies. And when you look at blessings and curses out of that Hebrew tradition from the book of Deuteronomy, that's what the prophets were saying, that God is not blessing this. God does not bless it—bless us.

When Martin Luther King, Jr. spoke out against the war, he was, in the words of Jeremiah Wright, "vilified." Wright recalls what most of us forget: "The year before [King] was assassinated, April 4th, 1967 at the Riverside Church, he talked about racism, militarism and capitalism. He became vilified. He got ostracized not only by the majority of Americans in the press; he got vilified by his own community. They thought he had overstepped his bounds."

A month after that sermon at Riverside, King gave a speech at a staff retreat in South Carolina where he said,

> In short, we have moved into an era where we are called upon to raise certain questions about the whole society. We are still called upon to give aid to the beggar who finds himself in misery and agony on life's highway. But one day, we must ask the question of whether an edifice which produces beggars must not be restructured and refurbished. That is where we are now. ... [We] must see now that the evils of racism, economic exploitation and militarism are all tied together. And you really can't get rid of one without getting rid of the other. ... Somebody must say to America, "America, if you have contempt for life, if you exploit human beings by seeing them as less than human ... you thing-ify those human beings. And if you thing-ify persons,

you will exploit them economically. And if you will exploit persons economically, you will abuse your military power to protect your economic investments and your economic exploitations." . . . The whole structure of American life must be changed.[27]

This is not, as Jeremiah Wright points out, the material of sound bites. This is not the oft-played and recalled excerpt from King's legendary "I Have A Dream" speech in 1963. This is the voice of a prophet wearied and largely ignored.

Near the end of King's speech at the staff retreat in May, 1967, he says,

> . . . [T]he prophets remind me, that somebody must bring God to man, and say "Thus sayeth the Lord." And Amos had it right, when God speaks, who can but profit from it? Isaiah and Jeremiah dealt with it . . . and I must confess the spirit of the Lord is upon me. . . . There are times in life when you must take a position that is neither safe nor politic nor popular. But you do it because it is right. . . . I want you to know that my mind is made up. . . . I will not be intimidated. I will not be harassed. I will not be silent and I will be heard.

The questions for us, dear sisters and brothers: Are we listening? Are we praying? Are we speaking truth to power? Or are we sitting comfortably in our seats?

Talk to your neighbors. Talk to your friends. Talk to the ones who least want to hear.

Today is May fourth. The anniversary of the killing of four unarmed college students shot by National Guardsmen on the campus of Kent State.

From first-century followers of a radical Jewish prophet to a presidential candidate who knows his electability depends

---

27 Martin Luther King, Jr., Speech at Staff Retreat, Frogmore, South Carolina, May 1967

on distancing himself from a contemporary one, the prophetic tradition summons *us* to decide, in the words of Ezekiel, whether we will "put away violence and oppression"—whether we will connect worship on Sunday to the anguished cry of the world on Monday—"and do what is just and right" (45:9). Context is everything.

Of Advent and Uncertainty

The days grow shorter. The light recedes. The sun melts into the horizon a bit earlier each day. We have another month until solstice, when we cross the shortest day and breathe into the lengthening again. Today marks the beginning of Advent in the Christian calendar, the start of the liturgical year. Nora Gallagher, a wise Episcopalian observer, writes that "in Advent, the holy breaks into the daily." Advent marks a season of waiting, a time of uncertainty, a period enriched by the fertile dark. A time ripe with anticipation, the seeds of something yet to come.

Outside, the squirrels have been preparing for quite a while; in deeply wooded regions, several species will hibernate, waiting in stillness for spring.

For many of us, the inevitability of winter is not a joy to behold. Snow and ice, fingers and toes that never stay warm, the rising cost of heat, the expansive hours of blackness that can feel like a shroud.

Unlike some of our sister creatures, we cannot hibernate in our dens. While German scientists have discovered two genes in humans thought to trigger hibernation, we are not yet ready to join the marmots and bears. And if we could curl ourselves into a ball, slow or suspend our breathing, and doze for months at a time, would we? Or is it intrinsic to our nature to remain conscious, to endure waiting without escape, to go so far as to listen to what the waiting reveals?

All of us must wait. We wait nine-plus months ourselves, and for our children, to be born. We wait for news from the doctor, the results of tests. We wait to recuperate—for infections and infirmities to subside. We wait for news of a scholarship, a promotion, a raise, disciplinary action, a verdict, a sentence. We wait for economic recovery. We wait for better jobs. We wait to meet the right mate. We wait for the mate we've met to get it right. We wait for the psychic wounds of childhood to loosen their grip. We wait for others to see the light, to recognize our truth, to come to their senses. We wait for politicians to act on our behalf. How much of our day is spent waiting? In traffic, in a queue, for the right opportunity, for sufficient courage to act, for adequate resources? Are our lives any less fraught with anticipation than the legendary figures of sacred stories?

The journey of Odysseus, the ascension of the prophet Mohammed up to the throne of God, a young woman named Mary, Noah and his family, Moses waiting to glimpse the Holy One. The stories seem grandiose but perhaps they merely reflect the enormity of our own waiting, the way we must sit in the palm of uncertainty, waiting as "the holy breaks into the daily." For in our waiting, the unknown jostles our illusion of security and mystery rings the edges of our routine.

Last week, a dear friend seeking settlement as a new minister awaited news. She had indicated her interest to several congregations. Poised by the phone for that exciting call, she received another one. Her twenty-one-year-old nephew in California, awaiting his own college graduation and wedding in May, suffered fatal injuries in a car accident. His parents flew in from Prague. The family gathered at his hospital bed and waited until they could wait no more. They unhooked life support and the young man died.

We wait to be born and we wait to die and though there are actuarial tables and all kinds of odds, we never know what awaits us even when we think we know what we are waiting for. Graduation, a new job, the start of a new life, a fresh relationship. Good news. Bad news. A letter, an email, a call, a knock at the door. Much as we plan, hope, anticipate, we can't be certain what awaits us.

I cannot help but think of my friend's brother and sister-in-law, on that flight to California from Prague, waiting to see their dying son. What was fertile in that darkness, in that eternity of ineffable grief? What is fertile in the darkness of our own winter? In the moments we wait to heal, in the moments we hope for a cure, in the days we seek respite, in the nights we long for relief?

It would make for a much easier sermon if I stuck to waiting out winter. If I filled the pages with interesting facts about how certain animals hibernate, painlessly waiting out the bite of winter for the song of spring. If I had only to reflect on the story of a young woman waiting to give birth to the son of God, of a world waiting in darkness for the light of the Lord. But here it is not that simple, and I suspect it was not so simple for writers of the Gospel accounts or Noah's tale in Genesis, nor was the waiting simple for Homer who told of Odysseus, or Mohamed in his revelations recorded as the Qu'ran.

The stark truth is that illumination is only visible relative to darkness. Spring manifests rebirth only in concert with the stillness winter brings. Only hopefulness and optimism create a context for disappointment and grief. And vice-versa.

We await news from the doctor, hoping to get well, to hear it was only a false scare. We await the second trimester of pregnancy before announcing it to be sure the pregnancy takes. We endure processes of transformation because we believe a fuller life awaits us on the other side of change. And like Mary and Odysseus and Noah and Mohamed, we set out on a journey encountering the unknown because that is what life requires. We pay for our admission ticket to life with our willingness to rise from our slumber and to sink back down into it, fully aware that we cannot know beforehand what light the darkness brings.

This we can know: that when trees outside appear bare, inside they are reinventing spring. None of us can apprehend at our own miraculous births how life will unfold—and when, where, and for how long we will be called upon to wait. But we can learn to inhabit our waiting with intention and purpose. We can memorize poems to recite when we stand in a long bank line.

We can count our blessings as we wait for that check to come. We can remind ourselves most of the time we have electricity as we wait for the power outage to end. We can sing songs as we sit in traffic or engage our senses as we wait for news. And we can let our hearts break open and pour out our sorrow as we wait to bid goodbye to someone we love. We can feel the full power of our rage and disappointment, we can grow faint with horror and grief. Waiting for the last pulse to drain from a life we hold dear, even our own, we can inhabit the present moment without forethought of the next one to come.

The Vietnamese Buddhist monk Thich Nhat Hanh tells us the real miracle is to walk on the earth, inhabiting this moment, especially when this moment feels patently infertile and horrifyingly dark. Somewhere it is still light. And that light, however distant, still spills into this universe, permeating every life. In the bitterest cold and blackest night, stars remind us that darkness gives birth to light. The deep pockets of earth that store bulbs, the amniotic sacs and eggs and marsupial pouches that gestate the young, the mind-boggling reaches of space that house billions of galaxies with their radiant stars—give the darkness its fertility.

We only think we are waiting. Even the bears understand hibernation is part of life. They know in the cells of their bodies all autumn as they carbo-load that their winter slumber is part of the life cycle. Suspended animation, but animation nonetheless. As they roll into a ball, tucking head between forepaws and turning heavily furred back to the cold, bears say *yes* to life. They, like us, have no guarantee they will survive, but this is what the moment calls for. Life on life's terms. Let us not confuse dormancy or stillness with death.

To everything there is a season, and a time to every purpose.

Our waiting, like the darkness, can be fertile, if we inhabit the stillness and uncertainty by fully engaging with what this moment offers instead of focusing on what the next moment will bring. To quote Pema Chödrön, "One of the most powerful Buddhist teachings is that as long as you are wishing for things to change, they never will. . . . As long as you are oriented toward the future, you can never just relax into what you already have or already are. . . . Instead of looking for fruition, we could just try to stay with our open heart and open mind. By entering into this kind of unconditional relationship with ourselves, we can begin to connect with the awake quality that we already have."

The most difficult part of this teaching for me is that sometimes being awake is painful. We all experience those moments we wish we could be numb. When I think of the most difficult times in my life, those moments of acute pain, grief, anguish, moments I would not wish on anyone, I know they are also the moments where transformation occurs.

Walking into hospital rooms as a chaplain; sitting with my dying father knowing he was not ready to die; waiting for months to hear the results of a committee's decision; driving somewhere to deliver bad news—we all have moments that wring us dry, that heave us onto shores of anxiety, even despair. Be it agony or ecstasy, it too shall pass. Each moment transforms into another one. No moment lasts. What feels like waiting is actually an irretrievable morsel of life.

The question of Advent is What will we do with our waiting? Will we inhabit it fully or pass the time in a state of anticipation? Will we dream of what the future may hold or remain awake even to what dormancy brings? In Christian churches, Advent services often involve "the play between the dark of winter and the frail light of candles" (Nora Gallagher). Such services ritualize truths only the earth can tell. In the planting of seeds, as we press our fingers into the ground, we can imagine blossoms to come, but we can also close our eyes and feel the miracle of soil right now, the generations and species of life palpable in each granular bit. The seeds themselves are not the only bearers of new life. The humus tells the story of life and death transformed; in every moment life remakes itself anew.

"In Advent, the holy breaks into the daily" because it is in our waiting that our lives are lived. Waiting, more than any other time or circumstance, invites us to inhabit the present moment just when we don't want to. Amid flirtations of the future or courtings of the past, we can choose to abide in the moment that holds us, even when it summons us to pain. The true miracle is not a virgin birth or a prophet's ascension into the heavens. It's not even the way a woodchuck or raccoon can suspend its breathing when it hibernates. The miracle happens when we know in our uncertainty, in our hunger to anticipate, in the grip of discomfort, or the delight of expectancy, that we are fully alive.

W. H. Auden writes,

> When the aged are reverently, passionately waiting
> For the miraculous birth, there must always be
> Children who did not specially want it to happen,
>   skating
> On a pond at the edge of the wood.

At the edge of the wood, as trees bare themselves and the stars come into view, the earth whispers: this is the moment we have been waiting for. Be in it, fully present and awake to the holiness it brings.

Little Boxes

This is one of those rare sermons where the title came first. A double entendre that calls to mind the Malvina Reynolds song: "Little boxes made of ticky-tacky, little boxes all the same." This time of year I think of little boxes, all those fabricated fancily wrapped ones that adorn display windows, meant to entice us to buy what we neither need nor want. When I was four, I remember being so disappointed the pretty boxes were empty, or worse yet, when I saw a colorfully wrapped package in my story book and carefully cut it out to see what was inside—well, let's just say it was my first lesson in the illusion of little boxes and what they contain.

But I am not just musing on gifts this morning, or packages of the tangible, wrap-able sort. I am speaking of the boxes we try to squeeze ourselves into—a bit like the old wedding dress or tux, or high school jacket that just doesn't fit who we have become. I think of these boxes this time of year because in addition to this being the season of Hanukah, solstice, and Christmas, it's also the season of grading. Students and teachers everywhere, especially in college and university, know that December is all about semester grades, and I can't think of little boxes I dislike more than the ones where the grade goes.

This week my college writing students turned in final papers. As much as I want the students to focus on what they learned, how critical thinking and clear writing will change their lives, most of them still race to a grade report and tear it open like the little box I tried to unwrap so many years ago. No doubt some students will experience the same crushing disappointment I did. My heart tugs for those students even if they are the masters of their own grade fate, but it tugs more for the students fulfilled by a pleasing grade. A part of me cringes knowing how easy it is to let a letter inside a little box define a feeling about the experience of learning.

I spent my junior year at Antioch College where there were no letter grades, only a pass/fail system with narrative evaluations written by both student and professor that provided much more comprehensive feedback and insisted on self-reflection. Ever since then, I have favored such a system and harbored a deep loathing for letter grades. For me, they are boxes I wedge my students' effort and performance into like a slender envelope into which a single snapshot will fit when what I want to evaluate is the entire roll of film documenting each student's learning process.

My frustration with little boxes is that so often they get in the way of imagination. And if we think about the holidays of the season, they all celebrate the act of imagination. Take for instance winter solstice, where our forebears brought greens into their dwellings to conjure the fecundity of life in the midst of darkest winter. Thousands of years ago, humans erected stone structures "built to receive shafts of sunlight on winter solstice." Powered by their imagination and determination, our forebears found ways to harness light.

Or consider Hanukah, which arose after Alexander the Great introduced Jews to Hellenistic culture. Some city-dwelling Jews assimilated, but many rural Jews who were farmers held fast to their ways and resented foreign rule and the Jewish elite who courted favor with their Greek conquerors. Burdened by taxation and repulsed by the Hellenists' love of power, a small band of rebels under the leadership of a country priest and his five sons, who came to be known as "the Maccabees," decided to fight back against imperialism. Though overwhelmingly outnumbered and outpowered, they believed the human spirit was more powerful than technology. In 165 BCE they retook Jerusalem, purified and rededicated the Temple (Hanukah means "dedication"), and rekindled the eternal light.

And then there is Christmas, which commemorates the birth

of Jesus, who like the Maccabees dared to imagine and embody an alternative power structure and a different way of living that favored intrinsic humanity over the boxes of categorization that his contemporaries used as zealously as we do. Jesus, as much as any historic figure on record, disregarded the boxes intended to reduce people to sinners or saints, lepers or Samaritans. As my friend and colleague in ministry Cricket Potter says, "Imagination leads us to beauty, possibility, and a life of exploration."

Imagination also summons us to a view beyond the horizon of what we know, what we have been told. Imagination demands that we see past the little boxes and the big box stores and the patterns of being that lead us if not into temptation, into stasis. Just this week, in an essay in *Newsweek* magazine, James Hansen, director of the NASA Goddard Institute for Space Studies, bemoans the inability of the president and Congress to imagine a realistic response to global warming. "Our planet," he writes, "is in imminent danger of crashing. Yet our politicians are not dashing forward. They hesitate, they hang back." That's not what the Maccabees did. They advanced against overwhelming force. It's not what Mary did as she assented to an angel or what her son Jesus did as he reimagined a religious landscape radically different from the one in which he was raised.

Sometimes, our lack of imagination imperils us. Other times, it just gets us in a jam, like one unfortunate student whose failure to imagine her way out of the box led her into the temptation to plagiarize. Imagine her, emailing me in tears after she received my email bearing the bad news. Busted for major swaths of stolen words, this after a warning on the second draft. Imagine me, grumpily confirming my suspicion, scrolling down the scholarly article she cited in some places and plagiarized in others. Can you hear my *harrumphing* as I clackity-tapped an email cutting and pasting the lifted text so that she see her transgression? I was not a happy grader because of course I want students to flourish. I want them to find their authentic voice, to use research to re-see the world and transform it through the synthesis of study and creative imagination.

And here's the irony: in a course entitled "How We Learn," in a paper arguing that standardized testing places students in little boxes instead of offering a useful assessment, the student wrote this after getting caught, "I have realized you are the type of teacher who isn't looking for this perfect student who can write like a pro; you're just looking for the students' voice and what they have to say, regardless of their skill level."

If only the student could have imagined the sufficiency of her own voice the way the poet Lisel Mueller imagines Monet's refusal to undergo eye surgery late in life. The poet writes:

Doctor, you say that there are no haloes
around the streetlights in Paris
and what I see is an aberration
caused by old age, an affliction.
I tell you it has taken me all my life
to arrive at the vision of gas lamps as angels,
to soften and blur and finally banish
the edges you regret I don't see,
to learn that the line I called the horizon
does not exist and sky and water,
so long apart, are the same state of being.

Why is it we so often prefer little boxes to "the vision of gas lamps as angels"? We revere Monet and his impressionistic cohort. We love them in part for seeing the world more clearly and more imaginatively than we do; yet we often cling to what we know. A. J. Jacobs, in his book *The Guinea Pig Diaries*, investigates dozens of biases of the brain. We are hard-wired to seek information that supports our beliefs and aligns with our own experience. Just as my student sought and found substantial evidence to support her position against standardized testing because she herself struggled with it (as did I), most of us gravitate toward that which reinforces instead of what transports. We usually prefer familiar ground to elsewhere, "to the edges of regret [we] don't see, . . . to learn that the line . . . called the horizon doesn't exist . . . that sky and water . . . are part of the same being."

Yet if we allow ourselves to notice all the little boxes, evaluative boxes—grades and ratings; descriptive boxes such as the M or F we have to check, married, single, partnered, divorced, widowed; Democratic, Republican, Independent, Conservative, Liberal, Progressive; Theist, Atheist, Humanist, Christian, Jew, Pagan, Buddhist, none of the above—we might decide to draw circles or spirals or the helix that doubles back on itself, because truly, none of us stay fixed in any moment in time. None of us exists on a stationary point. We are the pulsating fluid line that falls, rises, and entwines. And if, in our neurological natures, we lean toward the box, unfolding the customary carton, sliding ourselves in, we can pause in the midst of this season and recall the forebears who built stone structures to capture the light. We can shut our eyes and imagine them inventing possibilities they had not met before, and we can take heart.

We can call to mind the farming Maccabees who recoiled at urban sensibilities that shifted power. We can channel their courage and determination but also their capacity to envision life outside the Hellenistic box, a box fashioned to hold assimilation and relinquished ideals.

In the same way the scientist James Hansen beseeches us to conjure a planet with polar ice caps no longer melting, an atmosphere where carbon dioxide dips below 350 parts per million instead of climbing to four hundred, the nativity story beckons us to find not just our inner-conservationist, but our inner-traveler, the one who strides toward Bethlehem, guided by not only a distant star, but by a willingness to suspend disbelief, a welcoming of possibility. The poet Ann Reem writes, "When we are Bethlehem-bound / we can no longer look the other way / conveniently not seeing stars / not hearing angel voices."

Like Mueller conjuring Monet, we can take our rightful place beyond little boxes made of ticky-tacky or gaily festooned. We can allow our gaze and our creativity to surpass expectations. When I think of my student plagiarizing I realize she is far from alone. How many of us have mooched a clever line or passed off an idea as our own to impress someone at a party or a job interview? Many of us know firsthand the allure of borrowing mannerisms, affecting a witty gesture—not out of a conscious desire to co-opt, but out of a yearning to slip into a box labeled successful or charming, competent or conforming. I understand how my student could admit, "Some of the stuff I didn't quote and took from someone else just started to feel like it was my work." So often we do not suffer from a lack of conscience but rather a lack of imagination. If the student could imagine her words as fragments of light capable of illumination she could crawl right out of the box she fell into, deep down the rabbit hole.

And we, "Bethlehem bound," can point the way. Lisel Mueller conjures the wizened Monet, declaring,

> The world
> is flux, and light becomes what it touches,
> becomes water, lilies on water,
> above and below water,
> becomes lilac and mauve and yellow
> and white and cerulean lamps,
> small fists passing sunlight
> so quickly to one another
> that it would take long, streaming hair
> inside my brush to catch it. . . .
> Doctor,
> if only you could see
> how heaven pulls earth into its arms
> and how infinitely the heart expands
> to claim this world, blue vapor without end.

Here we are in the flux of the world, in the midst of Hanukah, little more than a week before Solstice, in the heart of Advent, earthen creatures blessed with the capacity to imagine ourselves translucent and shimmering, courageous and powerful, capable of great mischief and yet all the while able, should we choose, to free ourselves, in the words of Lisel Mueller, from "youthful errors: fixed notions of top and bottom / the illusion of three-dimensional space." Let this be the season we leave the little boxes behind.

Another Way

One of the things I love about Unitarian Universalism is the way it invites me, who grew up Jewish in the Bible belt of the South, occasionally assailed by the buckle, to find meaning in the Christmas season. In a couple of weeks, I'll ruminate on Nature's advent, by which I mean the lessons and gifts of the natural world in winter, but today, I continue with my effort to make meaning in the Christian story of Jesus entering the world. I like doing so because my earliest salvation came in the form of Logos—the written word; stories saved me as a child. The ones I made up, the ones I read, the ones that gave me another way of being in the world.

My friend Rich, who is finishing his last year at Union Theological Seminary in New York, just sent me a paper he wrote, entitled "The Jesus of Zen: According to Mark." In it, he explains, "Zen practice has enabled me to know the Messiah not by doctrine, but by experience. . . . Zen has given me words to express something I wanted to say so many times as a boy in my CCD classes but did not know how. That is, Christianity is *one* way of interpreting the events of Jesus' life. Christianity testifies to Jesus. Jesus does not testify to Christianity." For Rich, who grew up in a Catholic home in rural New Hampshire and has come to find much meaning and value in his Zen practice, he wishes to remain in dialogue with the New Testament. As he puts it, "That canon is where my spiritual life took root and grew from. The Gospels animated the holidays my family observed. . . . Neither religiously Catholic or culturally Zen, I am a cultural Catholic who practices Zen meditation."

Like Rich, I aspire to find that third way, not to be locked in the either/or dualism that sadly captures far too much of the American imagination this time of year. Just the other day, I met with a college writing student whose research paper focuses on the recent spate of live action films based on comic book characters. My student and I discussed the way these larger-than life-superheroes and villains fit right into a political backdrop where nations, leaders, and a billion Muslims are cast on or against an axis of evil, as if the world itself had become a Marvel comic.

It's easy to put up billboards reminding us "to keep Christ in Christmas" but useless if we don't meditate on the nuance overlooked by Rich's CCD teachers, who instructed him that "Jesus was the only Son of God [who] hoped [we] would enact legal restrictions on women's reproductive lives."

The poignancy of Jesus's human experience gets obscured by the singular rendering of his earthly life as somehow perfect. According to the gospel of Matthew, Jesus managed in utero to provoke King Herod, who, when he heard about the anticipated birth of Jesus, "was frightened, and all Jerusalem with him." Many of us are familiar with the story: Herod summons the wise men to learn the exact date and time of Jesus's birth, with the ruse that Herod wishes to pay homage to the newborn "king of the Jews." As the tale gets told, the three wise men reach the babe beneath the star and bring him gifts. "And having been warned in a dream not to return to Herod, they left for their own country by another road. "After the wise men depart, an angel appears to Joseph and instructs him to flee with his family to Egypt to escape Herod (Matt 2:12-13).

"When Herod saw that he had been tricked by the wise men, he was infuriated, and he sent for and killed all the children in and around Bethlehem who were two years old or under" (Matt 2:16). Herod also died after his rampage.

Herod, of course, gets painted as the megalomaniacal bad guy, and indeed his actions prove despicable. In an effort to derive a more instructive meaning, the great religious writer Kathleen Norris, an oblate among Benedictines, writes, "Herod symbolizes the terrible destruction that fearful people can leave in their wake if their fear is unacknowledged, if they have power but can only use it in furtive, pathetic, and futile attempts at self-preservation."

The gift of Ms. Norris's commentary lies both in her critical thinking and her compassion, the hallmarks of our liberal religious faith. She understands the narrative of Herod as allegory wherein Herod becomes the part of any of us when our fears go unchecked. While none of us here may be able to imagine having the power or the inclination to issue a genocidal decree as Herod did, I venture to guess that all of us have experienced moments when we misused the power at our disposal, out of fear, or rage, or grief. I still remember the moment I hoisted my then six-year-old sister up by the arms to bring her face to face. I knew instantly I had exerted my size and might out of frustration, no doubt with my own limitations as much as hers.

Who among us has not at least occasionally indulged in the excoriating word if not forceful touch? Who among us has not dismissed a person as summarily as Herod discounted the humanity of every Jewish male under two? Who among us has not abandoned the glimmer of possibility that our momentary interpretation of a situation, group, or individual could be incomplete?

I, for one, have allowed many moments to pass without acknowledging a third way, that plane of reality beyond right and wrong—this or that—where nuance and shading dwell. I get stuck more often than I wish to, though far less than I used to. My first teacher for this particular spiritual lesson was a man named Steve Scripter, whom I met in a writing class I taught in the protective custody unit of the men's prison in New Hampshire twenty years ago. Steve was a gentleman, an exemplar of courtesy and someone I would have invited to dinner had he not been incarcerated. After the six weeks of our class, on a lark, really, I stopped by offender records on my way out of the building. As a volunteer, I had access to the prisoners' files. For reasons I did not know or comprehend then, I sat at a table reading the files of each of the students. The criminal offenses of the others did not surprise me. The guy who plagiarized his papers from the pages of the encyclopedia was serving time for forgery, predictably enough. But when I got to Steve's file and realized he was serving time for rape, I literally felt the ground beneath me crumble.

How could someone I liked so much be a rapist? And it was Steve who taught me that I never wanted to refer to someone that way again. Certainly, he served seven-and-a-half years for rape, but I was unwilling to consign the totality of his being to a crime, no matter how horrific. To deny him his full humanity would diminish my own. Neither he nor I questioned his responsibility. I remember him telling me one day after he had been released, if he ever re-offended he should be put to death because he *knew* not to do it again. Steve Scripter did not re-offend. After release from prison, he moved back in with his parents, got work as a manual laborer breaking and carrying huge rocks. He reconnected with an old girlfriend and started rebuilding his life. At twenty-nine, he dropped dead, the day before Thanksgiving, of a massive heart attack.

Though it may seem even more of a stretch to some of you than my friend Rich's Zen interpretation of Jesus, I think of Steve Scripter, who also grew up Catholic in rural New Hampshire, as one of the many faces of the risen Christ, because he so clearly embodied what for me is the central teaching of Jesus: it is only in an uncondemned state that any of us can change. It was Steve who taught me the power, the truth, and the possibility of both/and instead of either/or.

He was a man who violated and terrified another person in inexcusable ways. He was a man courageous enough to transform himself from the angry husk of emptiness he had become into the fully human—that is to say broken and blessed—being I came to know and love.

Both realities are true. That's where the comic books and oversimplifications of Jesus and Herod and everyone in between mislead us, sending us down a path that dooms us because it veils the multiplicity of truths.

To confine Jesus to that classic Sunday School portrait loses the complexity. I wonder, as the bumpersticker says, what Jesus would have done, how he might have reacted to Herod's terrible decree had he faced it in adulthood. Might he have wondered what would drive Herod to such extremes? Would he have reflected, on his journey to see him, what Herod had faced as a boy or youth that had transformed him into such a power-hungry man? When he was summoned into Herod's chambers would he have invited Herod to reflect on the sources of his suffering? Maybe. Maybe not. Perhaps Jesus was prescient enough to foretell a bit of Zen.

Within Christian traditions, the anticipation of Jesus's birth symbolizes for many a period of fertile darkness wherein a different kind of possibility gestates. Or to borrow the words of poet Denise Levertov,

> We have only begun
> to imagine the fullness of life.
> How could we tire of hope?
> —so much is in bud . . .
> How might it be
> to live as siblings with beast and flower
> not as oppressors.

How might it be to see in those we condemn a possibility beyond our imagining?

How might it be to see in today's Herods "the terrible destruction that fearful people can leave in their wake if their fear is unacknowledged," and ask ourselves how *we* as much as *they* need to acknowledge our deepest fear? Our misuse of power?

Can we instruct by example as Jesus did?

Denise Levertov writes:

> there is too much broken
> that must be mended,

too much hurt we have done to each other
that cannot yet be forgiven.
We have only begun to know
the power that is in us if we would join
our solitudes in the communion of struggle.[28]

Life holds us in the palm of its complexity, its both/ands
and multiple truths. As humans, we engage with each other in
moments made intimate through disparate realities. Herod
is not a singular king in a singular historic moment. He is part
of a timeless story, as is Jesus, that enfolds our lives as well. A
story of power corrupted and power freed. A story of anger and
emptiness transformed into rage. But the story does not end
there. It continues in each reiteration, in what a Zen Jesus might
call Beginner's Mind, where we let go of everything we think we
know and open ourselves to "the fullness of life."

It is advent. The darkness sets early and lifts late. Outside, the
trees appear bare. Inside, they are reinventing spring.

---

28 "Beginners," *Candles In Babylon*

Evolution of Ideas

Thursday marks the bicentennial of Charles Darwin, and Abraham Lincoln's birth. Different though they and their influences were, both contributed to a tectonic shift in ideas. Neither arrived at his culminating treatise—Darwin's 1859 *The Origin of Species* and Lincoln's 1865 Emancipation Proclamation—in a vacuum. Both drew upon and subsequently enlarged, crystallized, and codified pre-existing ideas. Lincoln predicated his decision to end U.S. slavery on the existing framework of abolition built by many, and established in Britain in 1833, through tireless efforts of William Wilberforce. Darwin applied his keen observation and synthesis to the work of Alfred Russel Wallace, who "had developed an evolution theory similar to Darwin's but not as fully substantiated."[29]

These two men, each in his own way, demonstrate the evolution of ideas, underscoring that part of the evolutionary process, at least for humans, involves reckoning with tectonic ethical and intellectual shifts.

I am struck by this as I read the "My Turn" guest essay in this week's *Newsweek*, penned by Richard Mouw, the president of Fuller Theological Seminary in Pasadena, California. Fuller, an evangelical Christian, writes of himself, "I have spent several decades of my life trying to spell out an evangelical alternative to 'the worst kind of fundamentalism.' My friends and I have argued that the Bible supports racial justice, gender equality, peacemaking and care for the environment—views that often draw the ire from the worst kind of fundamentalists."[30] Mouw writes of his desire for respectful dialogue about Proposition 8,

---

29 Hayden, Thomas. "What Darwin Didn't Know." *Smithsonian*, Feb. 2009, p. 43

30 Mouw, Richard. "Less Shouting, More Talking." *Newsweek*, Feb. 9, 2009, p. 26

the recently passed ban on same-sex marriage in California. He supported the ban and fears its passage would lead to a "slippery slope." If we as a nation, in his words, "normalize" gay marriage, "what would keep us from extending marriage to a three-partner arrangement?"

During the four years I lived in Canada, where same-sex marriage is legal, I officiated close to two dozen ceremonies. No one approached me about a three-partner marriage, but to be fair to Mr. Mouw's concerns, there is a small group within Unitarian Universalism advocating for polyamory, which denotes a loving domestic relationship among more than two people. Admittedly, when I first spotted an ad in the *UU World* for a polyamorous organization, I cringed, along with several of my colleagues. Immediately I thought, *Oy*, how will we achieve respect from other denominations if we always house the fringe elements?

But the truth is, for me, that I wouldn't be standing here if it weren't for the fringe elements that paved my way. While there are slightly more female than male Unitarian Universalist ministers serving congregations today, that was not the case fifty years ago. And while I joke sometimes at UU minister gatherings that middle-aged women sporting comfortable shoes have taken over, I am indebted both to those who came before and the congregants now who care not, or perhaps appreciate, a female minister who finds her authentic fashion expression largely in the men's department.

As for polyamory, I found having one domestic partner challenging enough. I am one of those folks genuinely happiest living as a single person sustained by friendships, family, and work I love. For me, that is enough. But I appreciate the deep satisfaction and enrichment many people, gay and straight, find within marriage. The hopefulness, devotion, and delight I witnessed among gay couples perhaps exceeded that of the heterosexual couples whose weddings I presided over, precisely because the same-gender pairs who could finally marry legally in Canada came to it with such appreciation for the sanctity of the commitment and the communal recognition marriage brings. This is not to say, sadly, that two of the lesbian couples are already divorced. It is only to say that an idea that was unimaginable fifty or even twenty years ago has already entered the public imagination, and as my learned and wise mentor The Right Reverend John Shelby Spong told me, "Once something like gay marriage enters the public discourse it is only a matter of time until it becomes a reality."

So to Mr. Mouw, I can only suggest that part of our process of evolution is the flourishing of ideas, some of which, like species, will meet extinction quicker than others. Obviously, polygamy existed during the centuries known as "Biblical times," for it appears in several Biblical texts. Obviously homosexuality existed as well. Otherwise the author(s) of the books of Exodus and Leviticus, and the Apostle Paul, would not have felt compelled to denounce it. Homosexuality occurs naturally in about 10 percent of the human population and pops up in various other species as well. For thousands of years, some men have opted to have multiple wives, and in a few cultures, women have chosen multiple husbands. Were I to delve into anthropological research I would probably find some basis for multiple partners as a mechanism for increasing the likelihood of children, and the attainment of property, land, and status. Today's polyamorous Unitarian Universalists may seek something else: a broader base of intimacy; more adults to parent or share household responsibilities, or even something as mundane as loving, desiring two people at once.

If we pull back our lens to consider contemporary relational patterns in evolutionary time, this century with its ongoing conversation and political struggle about same-gender marriage,comprises a nanosecond of geologic time. With roughly six billion human inhabitants, the earth groans under the expectation that it must support us at the same time we deplete what we perceive as resources for our taking. Even if every same-gender couple seeking legal matrimony were to marry this year, and even if the pocket of polyamorous Unitarian Universalists could do the same (though I have no idea whether any of them would wish to), we as a species, and even as a subset of inhabitants of industrialized nations where polygamy and polyandry are illegal, probably would not experience a shift of *tectonic* proportion.

To our evangelical brothers and sisters who genuinely worry over human behavior they view as falling outside the scope of Biblical teaching, I extend compassion, because it cannot be easy to try to live ethically and non-hypocritically within the constraint of a literalist reading of texts that normalize polygamy and slavery, smiting entire communities, and individual punishments so severe it would be hard to honor and employ either our God-given or evolutionarily-endowed capacity for reason and abstract thought.

I don't say this smugly. To be a person of devout faith struggling to live in accordance with one's religious understanding describes me. In this way I have it easier: as a Unitarian Universalist, and as someone raised in a Reform Jewish home, I have never been saddled with literalism or a fundamentalism that declares me, my religious forebears, or fellow adherents the sole purveyor of truth.

That means as I, and we, enter the great evolution of ideas, we bring to the process not just the capacity but the predisposition to engage openly: to wade into the river, not to stand on its banks and assume we can direct its way. If we build a dam with our bodies we may redirect the flow—temporarily—but we cannot insist or insure that the next generation that replaces us as we tire or die will choose to dam the river in the same way.

In the centuries the various books of the Bible were written, marriage laws did not exist. The laws we recognize began as property rights for men. Few contemporary women would seek to enter into marriage as a covenant designed to clarify and insure a husband's right to her value and that of her possessions or land. The evolution of our idea of what marriage means has shifted radically in the last fifty years, and in the hundred before that. Faster than the blink of a geological eye.

> For forty years between 1932 and 1972, the U.S. Public Health Service (PHS) conducted an experiment on 399 black men in the late stages of syphilis. These men, for the most part illiterate sharecroppers from one of the poorest counties in Alabama, were never told what disease they were suffering from or of its seriousness. Informed that they were being treated for "bad blood," their doctors had no intention of curing them of syphilis at all.[31]

Today, the scientific community hangs its collective head in shame, or should. New standards are in place. And while today's public conversation about the ethics of primates and other mammals in scientific research may sound like people on the fringe, forty years ago there had to have been some folks somewhere saying it was not acceptable that the United States Public Health Department lied to economically disadvantaged African-American citizens to benefit more prosperous white ones.

Forty years from now, there may be a shift in collective sentiment. We may not publicly tolerate the use of animals in experimentation. We may not tolerate massive feed lots or the aerial killing of wolves. A hundred years hence, our children's children and their children may shudder at our barbarism. Fists and voices raised over the legality of same-gender marriage may seem passé.

Fifty or a hundred years from now, a sizeable number of people will still consult a sacred text—the Bible, the Qu'ran, the Bhagavad Gita, the Tao Te Ching, the Diamond Sutra—for guidance on right, and right-sized relations.

Because we never step in the same river twice, our descendents will likely arrive at different and differing answers.

---

31 Brunner, Borgna. "The Tuskegee Syphilis Experiment," www.tuskegee. edu

In the nineteenth and early twentieth century, when it was commonplace for impresarios and clinicians to place human beings with deformities or variations on view, few expressed outrage; many more paid to glimpse the display. Sideshows and so-called scientific displays of live human subjects are illegal, and those that might remain do so as remnants on the fringes of what the majority consider unethical. Still, a foray into the netherworld of cyberspace would undoubtably yield a trove of contemporary images.

This generation distances itself from the pseudo-science of the Third Reich with its racist applications of craniometry and eugenics. "In 1950, UNESCO issued a statement signed by leading researchers debunk[ing] race theories,"[32] yet tragically, that has not put an end to racism or theories of cultural superiority among many of the world's people.

What *has* changed is the emergence of a palpable shift in thinking. What previously functioned as viable intellectual currency has become the counterfeit bill of our day. In the same way forgery exists, at least most of us recognize it as such.

But that recognition emerges with time as both context and sensibilities change.

In early 2009, at the bicentennial of Darwin's and Lincoln's birth, same-gender marriage, reproductive technology, animal rights stand like boulders in the river of ideas. Well-intentioned people of varying perspectives wade into the river—some trying to dislodge the stones and send them hurtling downstream out of view; some working to transform the rocks of impasse into the sands that form the riverbed of common thought.

A hundred and fifty years after Darwin published *The Origin of Species* his theories hold—among most, but not all. A hundred and four, almost five, years after Lincoln signed the Emancipation Proclamation, the first African-American president occupies

---

32 http://en.wikipedia.org/wiki/The_Race_Question

the White House—to the delight of perhaps billions, and to the horror of white supremacists and apparently Rush Limbaugh. As tempting as it may be for religious liberals to shake our heads with incredulity at Biblical literalism, Creationism, the strident opposition to same-gender marriage, and perhaps most of all at the enormous following and political sway Rush Limbaugh has amassed, we can with humility recall, as the great African-American scholar Henry Louis Gates reminds us, Lincoln, even though he opposed slavery, considered "the Negro" intellectually inferior, unsuitable to serve in the military or marry a white person.

How, we might wonder, could someone who progressively changed history be drawn into the undertow?

Our evolution as humans, as Lincoln and Darwin so poignantly and eloquently demonstrate, entails the evolution of ideas: not just thoughts, but critical and compassionate thinking, the ability to investigate, weigh, and synthesize multiple perspectives and contexts. The variations—of species *and within* our own—promise and demand nothing less.

Look to See
Who is There

An Act of the Recklessly Generous Heart

Though it may seem an odd association, when I think of hospitality, September 11, 2001, comes to mind. On that fateful day, I was vacationing with family in Scotland. We began the day as we had the two or three before, enjoying a hearty breakfast at the farmhouse B&B where we were booked through the night of the 11th, due to fly home on the 12th. We learned of the morning's horrific events from a cashier in a Scottish heritage museum gift shop. It was what I call "a before and after" day, the events of which are so profound the date becomes a marker of irreparable change. When we returned to the farmhouse, we were met at the door by our innkeeper, Catriona, whose husband Hugh ran the small family farm with his father, uncle, and two brothers. In addition to keeping up the bed and breakfast, Catriona helped out on the farm, raised two active young sons, and drove a small school bus. To be sure, that Tuesday afternoon she had her hands full, yet she met us with open arms.

She asked if we knew what had happened; we told her we did.

She ushered us in, made us a pot of tea. Brought the phone from the kitchen into the living room. Told us to use the computer in the kitchen as well. She told us she'd call the couple who'd booked for the weekend and tell them they'd have to reschedule. "You can stay as long as you need. And don't worry about paying."

Over the next five days and nights we stayed, Catriona shared the stew from their dinner and made us sandwiches at lunch. She refused any offer to pay for calls or use of the computer and she took us to the little village church that Sunday, where her mother-in-law gave us the altar flowers so that we had something pleasant to focus on.

Before we left, the four of us went into town to the cash machine and withdrew enough to pay for the extra days. We knew Catriona did not expect it and we knew we would never leave without giving it to her. In truth, we could never repay her hospitality. The way she opened her home to us, gave extravagantly of her time and energy, offered compassion and comfort in the midst of a world seemingly blown apart.

We could not sort out terrorism, bad foreign policy, people under siege. We could not open the airspace above the U.S. or book a flight home. We could not console the thousands in shock or grief. We could not even agree amongst ourselves who bore responsibility for the events of September 11—who was complicit, who was to blame. Tensions in my family mounted amidst the stress and uncertainty. And in that quagmire, the gift of Catriona's hospitality reminded us, at a time when it would have been hard to believe, that maybe, just maybe, Anne Frank had been right when she wrote shortly before her death at the hands of the Nazis that in spite of everything, people are really good at heart.

When we have nothing, not even the certainty of survival, we can still offer each other hospitality. It is the one gift that does not require certainty or means. I've noticed, in fact, that it is often those who have the least in terms of material possessions or financial resources who offer the most gracious and generous hospitality. I remember sitting in the home of a Mexican woman whose six-year-old sold candy in the streets to support their family while she sold roses. Several of us visiting Mexico from North America sat on every available surface in the tiny room lit only by a crude opening in the wall that served as a window. No screen, no glass. No electrical lights. A curtain divided the living room from the modest sleeping quarters, where she and her husband, her brother, and her children would crowd together at night. The six-year-old offered us candy, taking from the day's meager profits by giving it away to us. And when we left, the woman gave us each a rose from the single bundle she would later try to sell.

What accounts for this radical hospitality? Perhaps for the

woman in Mexico, the teachings of Jesus—who according to gospel accounts not only preached but exemplified radical hospitality. Jesus dined with prostitutes, tax collectors, the ill, and the shunned. Many of us have heard the oft-quoted sentiment attributed to Jesus, "If asked for your coat give your cloak as well," but there's more to it. The part that makes hospitality radical, that returns us to the root of its expression, comes in the full statement Jesus makes: "If anyone sues you to take away your coat, give him your cloak as well."

If anyone sues you—This is not simply a case of "Gee, I have three winter coats and I guess I could loan one even though I have a sentimental attachment to it." Jesus is not suggesting we root around in the closet for what no longer fits and give it to a friend, or even a stranger. He's saying give that cloak that you happen to like very much to the person who just sued you for your coat. Lest we think this a particularly Christian message, it harkens back to the Jewish imperative of *tzeduchah*, committing a righteous act; the third pillar of Islam, *zakat*, giving alms to those in need; and it corresponds with the Buddhist concept of Right Action. In a teaching uncannily similar to that of Jesus, the Buddha said when you are angry at someone, if you have tried everything else and still feel angry, practice generosity.

It's easy for any of us to get entrenched, to allow ourselves to act out of fear. To let our resentments or insecurities guide us. The fear we may express might be *What if we open the door to the stranger and he overstays, or eats us out of house and home?* But perhaps the greater, unarticulated fear is that *the stranger will introduce us not only to unfamiliar ways, but to our truest selves.*

In that way, every stranger comes bearing a gift. Every stranger or friend or family member or enemy in search of hospitality invites us to become acquainted with our best selves. If someone had asked a hard-working farm woman, "Would you like to have four stressed-out strangers stay an extra five days in your home and, by the way, would you like to spread the stew a little thinner and change the linens five more times and have them bustle about in your kitchen making tea and toast whenever they'd like?," would she have said, "Oh yes, sign me up?"

Probably not. But given the opportunity to do just that, she offered graciously, and as much as we received and appreciated her kindness, we also gave her that chance to extend radical hospitality, to find in herself stores of generosity, energy, and compassion she otherwise might not have accessed that week. So that's something to remember: that radical hospitality invites us to find and express our best selves.

Hospitality is about making people feel welcome. I think of my friend Kathleen, who is quadriplegic. She literally lives either in her motorized wheelchair or her bed, yet she has a living room and dining room full of beautiful furniture she will never sit in. It is for her guests. So why did she invest in such nice furniture instead of scrounging about at yard sales for any serviceable table or chairs? Because Kathleen wants her company to be comfortable. To feel valued. The first time she invited me to dinner, she cooked it by using my hands, her recipe, and her directions. I may have been the one lifting the fork to her mouth but she was the one feeding me.

Hospitality invites us to live out a human impulse that transcends cultural borders, religious differences, and the limits of resources or health. It allows each of us to be fully human and truly generous by occasioning the opportunity to be present and share our selves.

I think of the two seasons, once when I was fifteen and again at twenty-three, when I lived with my cousins, who expected no payment for room and board. I think of my cousin who shared her room, of my aunt and uncle who treated me as one of their children when my own parents were self-involved and unavailable. It was not just lodging and meals they gave me, but a sense of welcome, of belonging, of acceptance. They made me feel as though my presence enriched them. That is radical hospitality.

When Jesus and his disciples feed the multitudes with just a few loaves and fishes, it's an allegorical story worth listening to. When we add a few more carrots and potatoes or another cup of broth to the stew, we act on the faith of abundance even if our experience is one of scarcity, and that's the miracle. That we act on the belief that our generosity will sustain us. That our hospitality will nourish us. Long after our bellies quit rumbling, we will hear the sound of satisfaction that derives from knowing we have found and offered our best selves.

It is not the condition of our building, the lavishness of our surroundings, the elegance of the food we offer, or even the quality of our thought that welcomes others into our midst; it is that heartfelt expression of gratitude for the chance to practice kindness and hospitality.

Some congregations offer sanctuary to refugees or shelter people without homes. Not every congregation is equipped to do that, but every congregation can offer sanctuary to people seeking to be part of a religious community. We do it by welcoming each other with the mindfulness that it is our good fortune to be able to extend hospitality. What makes hospitality a spiritual act, no matter what religious or philosophical perspective we have, is that whether we offer it or receive it, we reap the benefit of experiencing it by coming into contact with human graciousness—by being reminded that in spite of everything people are really good at heart.

Radical hospitality invites us to reach beyond our comfort zones. In words reminiscent of Jesus and the Buddha, Joan Chittister says, "I cannot go on thinking that nodding to neighbors in the parking lot is hospitality. I cannot fool myself into thinking that being nice to those who are my kind and class suffices for the moral dimensions of hospitality. . . . No, hospitality is the willingness to be interrupted and inconvenienced so that others can get on with their lives as well."

In a Scottish farmhouse, a woman opens her arms and her home to travelers reeling from a world gone awry. In a Mexican shanty, a child passes a box of sweets and his mother gives nine women wealthy enough to fly to Mexico a rose. In Tennessee, a family of six becomes a family of seven for a while, and in each case a miracle as prosaic as kindness and as precious as generosity unfolds.

Beyond Acceptance Into Welcome

Many of our Unitarian Universalist congregations engage in a process to become a Welcoming Congregation. The United Church of Christ has a similar designation called Open and Affirming. The intention and effort of liberal religious congregations to embrace transgender, gay, lesbian, and bisexual members is so important because of the long history of exclusion, condemnation, and silencing that has taken place within religious communities. As we make strides toward inclusivity it's useful to ask what it means to be welcoming when we already feel accepting. Often, our congregations include lesbian, gay, and bisexual folks with relative ease. Sometimes the transgender part gets people in the trickbag, because gender is the primary way we sort the world. It used to be when a baby was born the first question would be "Boy or girl?," but now the question begins at amniocentesis or with the prenatal ultrasound. We orient around gender so if we can't discern a person's gender, either because that person's gender identity is deliberately fluid or just doesn't align with the cues we look for, it can throw us off. Transcending the boundaries of gender challenges our assumptions in the way same-gender marriage begs the question Why is marriage, a socially constructed institution, *inherently* reserved for one man and one woman? As a denomination we have taken a stance that the covenant of marriage belongs to those willing to commit to the challenge and joy of intimacy coupled with responsibility over the long haul. But that doesn't mean as individuals we all arrive at the gates of welcome.

How do we get below the surface of acceptance and respectful rhetoric to the depths of what unsettles us?

I never had a problem with gay people until I identified as one. Let me pause here to say there was a time in my life, in my

179

late teens and early twenties, when I was busy plastering "Lesbian Nation Is Rising" stickers on toilet seats, when I would have scolded myself for applying "gay" to women, which I was busy spelling with a "y". But now that I actually lovingly refer to myself as post-queer (which just means it is the culture I grew up in and identified with but the identity no longer contains me) I find it easier to just use gay for all varieties of queer folk, because why not be happy?

I am at the happy stage in my life where I understand the importance of language, the value of naming oneself and claiming one's own identity—*and* I have learned all words are metaphors for what the body experiences, and while they matter, they are portals to understanding but not understanding itself. The words we sing, the words we use to name elements of worship matter to each of us. But ultimately the words we use dissipate; hopefully what lingers will be what the words evoke.

So how do we dig deeper to understand what challenges any of us about being welcoming to folks who don't fit neatly on the gender spectrum or who partner with members of the same gender? Perhaps by acknowledging that welcoming anyone who is different in any way can be hard. Welcoming a vegan to Thanksgiving dinner or our barbecue-loving, McDonald's-craving friend to the locavore gluten-free recipe swap can be just as challenging as figuring out what pronoun to use when someone you've known as male transitions to female or vice-versa. Inviting folks who express a love of God to feel welcome in a primarily humanist Unitarian Universalist congregation can be far more taxing than flying the rainbow flag.

Most of us are comfortable with differences that don't challenge or abrade our own identity, or don't require us to step outside of our comfort zones. Well-heeled folks who know how to read and recognize the names of NPR hosts usually fit in here whether we are gay or not. Skin tone matters less than whether we sport a little Darwin fish or the other kind that means Jesus on the rear end of an energy efficient car.

But that's where welcoming exceeds acceptance. Welcoming refers to the virtue of hospitality articulated beautifully in the sixth-century monastic Rule of St. Benedict: "All guests who present themselves are to be welcomed as Christ, who said: 'I was a stranger and you welcomed me.' . . . Once guests have been announced, the prioress and the community are to meet them with all the courtesy of love. . . . The prioress shall pour water on the hands of the guests, and the prioress with the entire community shall wash their feet."

Taken a step further, the great Sufi poet Rumi writes in his poem, "The Guest House":

> This being human is a guest house.
> Every morning a new arrival.
>
> A joy, a depression, a meanness,
> some momentary awareness comes
> as an unexpected visitor.
>
> Welcome and entertain them all!
> Even if they're a crowd of sorrows,
> who violently sweep your house
> empty of its furniture,
> still treat each guest honorably.
> He may be clearing you out
> for some new delight.
>
> The dark thought, the shame, the malice,
> meet them at the door laughing,
> and invite them in.
>
> Be grateful for whoever comes,
> because each has been sent
> as a guide from beyond.[33]

---

33 Translated by Coleman Barks, in *The Essential Rumi*

Obviously Rumi speaks metaphorically of the emotions, situations and conditions that arrive unbidden. "The dark thought, the shame, the malice—meet them all at the door laughing and invite them in."

I mentioned earlier I never had trouble with gay folks or the concept of queerness until I claimed that identity myself at seventeen. In 1993 when I attended a large rally in Washington for gay rights and saw bare-chested women congregating on a D.C. street corner, when I saw gay male S&M advocates marching in studded collars and leather thongs, I cringed. I wanted all the freaky way-too-out-there queers to go home and stop scaring the nice Midwesterners who had unwittingly brought their kids to see the nation's capitol on the wrong weekend.

My own internalized homophobia reminded me of the internalized anti-Semitism I felt several years before, in 1980 when I stood outside an auditorium in Connecticut, waiting for a Klezmer music concert to begin, wishing all the loud Jews with New York accents would disappear so no one would ever associate me with one of them.

I grew up in the South, where ill-informed children used to call me a Christ-killer because I was Jewish. As a defense against their ignorance, I took on a line I heard on a quirky TV show called "Mary Hartman," where a character said, "It was your people killed our Lord." Before anyone could ever hurl the epithet of Christ-killer at me again, I would say, "I know, I know, it was my people killed your Lord."

I used the line facetiously until finally, in the summer of 2000, my colleagues in Clinical Pastoral Education challenged me. They were all compassionate respectful Christians who knew historically Jews had not killed Jesus, so they asked me why I used my silly line defensively when there was no offense anymore. And that got me thinking. What I came to understand was that in the face of genuine discomfort at being accused of something I could not have done, I recognized the way I could have.

When I thought back to my contempt at all the loud pushy Jews I'd ever encountered, and the way-too-out-there queer folk who messed it up for the rest of us, I thought: who was Jesus but a loud pushy Jew who drew attention to himself all the time?

Since childhood, I have aligned with the downtrodden, the scorned, the misunderstood.—as long as they weren't loud, attention-drawing types. So if somehow I were surrounded by an angry mob, ready to send a noisy Jewish agitator to his death, could I conceive of the possibility that I might see the Roman equivalent of a billy club headed my way and yell in fear, and perhaps a bit of contempt, "Crucify him"? Yes.

In the Spanish film *La Mariposa*, a young boy develops a great fondness for his teacher, a Communist sympathizer, like the boy's father, under Franco's rise to power. At the end of the film, when the teacher and several others are arrested and dragged into the street, the boy's mother fears for her family's safety and instructs her son to yell "Reds" as the handcuffed men file by. The boy, emulating the adults around him, picks up a rock and hurls it at his beloved teacher. In that moment when I both hate the mother and identify with her, I recognize the Christ-killer and the homophobe in myself.

When I get so angry at Fred Phelps and his followers—who were in Washington at that rally in 1993 with their "God Hates Fags" signs just as they are at military funerals today, when I wrack my brain to understand how anyone can conflate God with hate or the word "fags," I know I have to heed Rumi and ask: What can the meanness and malice of Fred Phelps teach me?

That I am scared of what appears to undermine and therefore threaten me. That I am quick to dismiss Fred Phelps as a homophobic fundamentalist whack-job, but the moment I do, I diminish his humanity as quickly as he diminishes mine. Fred Phelps summons me to find the part of myself that bolts the door when I see the studded-collar leather-thonged men and my bare-breast-waving sisters coming.

The people at that rally I wished to distance myself from make me look run of the mill with my classy ties and Doc Marten shoes. I grew up convinced I was a boy in an erroneously female body and my parents indulged that. They let me wear boys' clothes and live in my own gender-reconstructed world. They may not have welcomed my queerness but they embraced me and were proud of me and never distanced themselves from a daughter who first longed to be their son and then went marching off to join some nascent lesbian nation that never rose.

To be honest, I would not cozy up to my strident twenty-year-old self. But I would go back and cradle her the day a fifteen-year-old student in remedial reading class where I assisted literally leapt across the room, squealing in horror after she asked me, "Are you gay?"

I thought hard how to answer the girl, knowing the truth would elicit that kind of response. Living our truths demands courage no matter who we are. Nowadays, being a tie-wearing female Jewish Unitarian Universalist minister probably wouldn't cause any of our congregations to bolt the door; but if I were to announce that deep in my heart I harbor an inner tent-revivalist who longs to bring Pentecostal fervor to liberal religious theology, some folks might jerk away the welcome mat.

"Treat each guest honorably" Rumi instructs, for each is "a guide from beyond."

To be welcoming means that we ask, and honestly answer. Which visitors trouble us? The ones who look scruffy, smell unkempt, or praise the Lord? The ones who challenge a neuro-typical view of the world? The ones who "go too far" with ethical veganism and PETA protests? Or the ones who wouldn't know what PETA stands for? To be welcoming, not just accepting, means that we sit down with the guy in the studded collar and the woman we used to know as a man; that we explain to our precocious children not just that some kids have two mommies or two daddies but that some kids have parents who place a sign that says "God Hates Fags" into their small hands. And they do it not because they are mindless bigots but because they fear what they have to lose. Perhaps they fear for the rest of us, or fear for the world they see slipping away. To be *welcoming* is to welcome every guest as a guide from beyond—which means if our doors remain open, we are life's perpetual students. To be welcoming summons us all to ask what it means and what it takes for the *guest* among us to become *one of us*. To be welcoming is to open the door and look in the mirror.

Freedom From Constraint

Passover begins today. At Seder tables everywhere, we retell the story of the Exodus. The introduction to the Haggadah, or book of service I use, begins: "This holiday commemorates the liberation of the Hebrew people from slavery in Egypt. Over the centuries its significance has broadened to include the desire for freedom among all people."

As a child growing up in Tennessee, I would sit at my cousins' table year after year, hearing the story retold of the Hebrew escape from slavery. The rest of the days of the year I was far more attuned to the centuries of slavery that had shaped and bloodied the U.S. South: that of Africans brought to America, millions of men and women captured, bound, sold, dehumanized. Though no one drew the connection at the Seder, it lurked in the room, a silent witness to the proceedings.

I had a science teacher in fifth grade, Mr. Berg, who instructed us to crawl under our desks. At that time, the only faces of color in the school belonged to the two custodians. Mr. Berg waited while we, the privileged white children of well-heeled professionals, schooched under our desks, tucking our bodies between the four metal legs. Mr. Berg sought to instruct us experientially, to give our bodies the slightest hint of how it would feel to be as confined as the millions of Africans had been during what was known as the Middle Passage, where as many as twenty million died and the ones that survived being chained together at sea for months arrived to a walking death, a soul-defying period in American history.

Today, some twenty-seven million people worldwide suffer contemporary forms of slavery, ranging from bonded laborers, many of whom are children, to females consigned to the burgeoning sex slave market. Writer Benjamin Skinner chronicles this in his new book, *A Crime So Monstrous: Face to Face with Modern Day Slavery*. Sadly, perhaps sinfully, slavery and the systemic oppression of certain peoples still stain the pages of our history as it is being written.

As Ruth Kletnick, a Jewish teacher I know, writes in her version of the Haggadah,

> Slavery did not end in Egypt. Many people have been slaves and many have been oppressed since then—people of different backgrounds, ideas, and faiths. Each of us is a slave to some degree, even today. We are slaves when we are not free to be ourselves, either from outside oppression or from our own inhibitions. We are slaves when we are silent, while injustices, even atrocities happen to others.

We are slaves when we are silent, while injustices, even atrocities happen to others.

It is this awareness that allows us to understand that people of privilege are not free from oppression. The effects of oppression—occupation, racism, war—vary greatly from perpetrator to victim, from unintentional collusion and silent complicity to being chained in bondage. But no one escapes unscathed.

Hence Martin Luther King, Jr's famous line, "Injustice anywhere is a threat to justice everywhere." No one is free until all are free.

There is a moment of this mindfulness built into every Seder during the recitation of the ten plagues visited upon the Egyptians; for each plague a drop of wine is removed from the cup—a recognition that the liberation of the enslaved Hebrews brought suffering to their oppressors, especially those ordinary citizens who were bound by a system they did not create but helped sustain, that rendered everyone less than whole. Any and each act of dehumanization is complete—dehumanizing both the dehumanized and the dehumanizer.

In divinity school as I reread the Torah portions that tell of the

Exodus, I stumbled again and again over these lines: "The LORD said to Moses . . . I 'will harden Pharaoh's heart.'" After the first plague where God turns the water to blood, the fish die, the stink overtakes the land, and there is nothing to drink, and Pharaoh's heart remains hardened. Next come the frogs that fill the ovens and kneading bowls so that there can be no cooking. No change in Pharaoh's heart. The gnats and flies follow, and then disease that overtakes all the livestock that belong to the Egyptians. Next come boils that fester on human and animal alike. The almighty Yahweh who brings forth such suffering surely could have softened Pharaoh's heart, but instead it grows harder. The LORD rains down thunder and hail, shattering every tree, striking every plant and animal and each Egyptian. Finally, Pharaoh says, "This time I have sinned; the LORD is in the right and I and my people are in the wrong. . . . I will let you go; you need stay no longer." But Moses replies, "I know that you do not yet fear the LORD God," and as if to prove the point, God hardens Pharaoh's heart yet again, telling Moses, "I have hardened his heart and the heart of his officials, in order that I may show these signs of mine among them."

This is, no doubt, what gives God a bad rap. Certainly the Greek pantheon is full of power-hungry and power-sated gods eager to demonstrate their prowess on mere human beings; still, we ask, Why did ancient scribes render a portrayal of a God so intent on proving his might? After the eighth plague—locusts—God once again hardens Pharaoh's heart. Then comes "the darkness over the land of Egypt, a darkness that can be felt." Finally, God tells Moses, "I will bring one more plague upon Pharaoh and upon Egypt; afterwards he will let you go from here." There can be no plague more chilling: "Every firstborn in the land of Egypt shall die, from the firstborn of the Pharaoh who sits on his throne to the female slave who is behind the handmill, and all the firstborn of the livestock. Then there will be a loud cry throughout the whole land of Egypt, such as has never been or will be again."

Reading those words sends a particular chill through me, having heard such a cry in my own family the day my firstborn brother died. What kind of message is this? It is not just Pharaoh and his officers who suffer, or even their children, in the way that early Hebrew writers believed the sins of the father would be visited on their children. No, even the female slave and the animals, the most powerless creatures in Egypt, are made to suffer because God has hardened Pharaoh's heart so that God can display his omnipotent and discerning wrath. "Not a dog shall growl at any of the Israelites."

I do not pretend to know what the early compilers and writers of this famous narrative sought to convey, other than a very human need for unstoppable vengeance. Understandably, long-oppressed people may need a narrative of retribution that exceeds the bounds of fairness, justice, or compassion. But beyond this lies a narrative of instruction for us, lo these millennia later.

In the land of oppression—in a land of war— everyone suffers. The enslaved Hebrews and the enslaved Egyptians suffer the indignities of bondage while the Pharaoh and his officials are captivated—held captive—by their own power. The animals, trees, and plants, even the swarms of insects and frogs suddenly too numerous to control, succumb to the frenzy. The land, the ground of all being, yields only the stench of death. While it appears that the Israelites flee unscathed, at least in the Exodus, thousands of years later, their descendants remove drops of wine from a glass "to temper our joy with sorrow for the Egyptians who died."

What can we glean from a story recited for a hundred generations where God hardens Pharaoh's heart again and again?

The story, with all its gruesomeness, compels us to examine the ways we harden our own hearts. Returning to Ruth Kletnick's version of the Haggadah, "We are slaves when we are silent, while injustices, even atrocities happen to others." As disturbing as it is to imagine God choosing to harden Pharaoh's heart instead of softening it, we are left to reckon with hardening our own hearts to the suffering we inflict through the vast disparity of resources, the wanton indulgences of a few, the skepticism over global warming, the quick reassurances about mountain top mining and hydrofracturing shale gas, the shrugs of our shoulders as more species become extinct as a result of our actions.

We live in a world where "not a dog shall growl" at many of us, yet if we listen, we can hear the growls and cries throughout the land. It is not just former UN envoy Stephen Lewis or the economist Jeffrey Sachs whose testimony reveals the ugliest of truths: that genocides and famines, earthquakes and hurricanes, epidemics and drought disproportionately affect people of color. The starvation, disease, inequity, poverty, and civil warfare in non-Anglo, non-European, or non-Western nations and communities are beyond compare.

In his book *Faith Without Certainty: Liberal Theology in the 21ˢᵗ Century*, Unitarian Universalist theologian Paul Rasor writes, "At several points during the past two centuries, religious liberals were led by their own convictions into stances that made them less effective advocates for racial justice than they might have been."

Rasor goes on to describe how our "ambivalence around issues of race persisted into the twentieth century." African-American theologian James Cone writes: "Whites do not like to think of themselves as evil people or to believe that their place in the world is due to colonization of Indians, the enslavement of blacks, and the exploitation of people of color around the world. Whites like to think of themselves as honorable, decent, and fair-minded people." Cone says, "Black anger upsets only whites who choose not to identify with black suffering." Both he and Rasor acknowledge "white liberals tend to be more comfortable in conversations that are more intellectual than emotional." As Cone points out, "Progressive whites do not mind talking as long as it doesn't cost much, as long as the structures of power remain intact."

But the story and commemoration of Passover call upon us to "suffer with." In fact, many traditional Seders begin with the instruction to listen not as people centuries removed but as slaves still living in Egypt.

The Hebrew word for Egypt is *Mitzrayim*, which comes from a word meaning narrow or confined. Egypt becomes our metaphor for places of confinement or narrowness. Thus Passover compels us to ask ourselves, What *Mitzrayim* must we leave in order to liberate ourselves? As Ruth Kletnick writes in the introduction, the Haggadah she has compiled, "When we speak of the story of Passover being a story of liberation from *Mitzrayim*, we are talking about Passover being a celebration of freedom from narrowness and constrictedness for anyone." And to that I would add, *everyone*.

In a book titled *Soul Work: Anti-Racist Theologies in Dialogue*, Unitarian Universalist minister Rosemary Bray McNatt writes of a conversation she had with Coretta Scott King, who attended Unitarian churches with her husband. McNatt recalls with great sadness Mrs. King telling her they had given a lot of thought to becoming Unitarian but realized they could never build a mass movement of black people as Unitarians. McNatt notes, "Certainly . . . race would have been the primary barrier" in a denomination that "until the 1970s, actively discouraged people of color from joining its ministerial ranks." She cites an essay of Dr. King's called "Pilgrimage to Nonviolence," wherein he writes,

> I came to feel that liberalism had been all too sentimental concerning human nature and that it leaned toward a false idealism. . . . Liberalism failed to see that reason by itself is little more than an instrument to justify man's defensive ways of thinking. Reason, devoid of the purifying power of faith, can never free itself from distortions and rationalizations.

We have all heard far too many distortions and rationalizations in the last several years. As wars continue with no end in sight, the death counts grows, the damage exponentially spirals, and a cry continues to fall across the land.

To the parent who wails in agony at the loss of a child, to the donkey that brays its grief, to the trees that splinter from the pelting of ammunition, to the earth that cracks from longer and longer droughts, to the riverbeds that run red with blood, oppression remains part of an ongoing story.

Let us hear the story as *participants*, not observers. *We are slaves when we are silent, while injustices, even atrocities happen to others.*

Let us be challenged and our hearts be *softened* by the conflicting realities of oppression. As we consider constraints that confine us, ways of being that inhibit us and keep us from spiritual wholeness, may we recognize today's plagues come not from an angry God, but from the choices we make.

Let us begin together to name and dismantle our *Mitzrayim*. For only by reckoning with the narrow places that bind us will we glimpse the Promised Land.

The Burden of Cain

The flags flew at half-staff till Wednesday for the men and women who died in the rampage at Fort Hood. In what became the bitterest of ironies, soldiers scheduled for or recently returned from deployment were gunned down on home base. The flags lowered to memorialize them melded into Veterans Day—a poignant reminder as one sign posted near Fort Hood reads: "In war there are no unwounded soldiers."

Cynthia Thomas, who runs a private assistance center for soldiers in Killeen, Texas, told the *New York Times*, "Whether it's self-medicating, anger or violence, these are the consequences of war, and you have to think about all the people affected by soldiers coming home, the parents, spouses, children, brothers, sisters, aunts and cousins."

War waged for any reason guarantees bitter consequences. As one combat reporter puts it, "war is about one thing: bullets meeting bodies." So how do we as humans reconcile our horror at the Fort Hood shootings with the reality that military training prepares soldiers to kill in the course of duty? Under what conditions does the premeditated or preconceived violent death of a human being change from a criminal act a to valorous one? When it intends to bring about liberty or stave off terror, in contrast to wanton destruction? We are not privy to the minds of those who randomly open fire, who target the innocent, the unsuspecting. But noted forensic psychiatrist James Gilligan, in his book *Violence: Our Deadly Epidemic and Its Causes*, writes, "even the most 'insane' violence has a rational meaning to the person who commits it. . . . *[A]ll violence is an attempt to achieve justice.*" Gilligan cautions that violence cannot be prevented until it is understood, and as such we must see all violence as tragedy.[34]

What does it mean to see all violence as tragedy?

Last weekend provided me with a glimpse.

I spent Friday evening and the better part of Saturday and Sunday co-facilitating an Alternatives to Violence Project Workshop at the men's prison in Shirley. During one activity we paired up, each person facing another, alternating speaking and listening. The facilitator leading the exercise called out instructions. "What do you wish you could be forgiven for?" I gazed at my partner. He leaned into his answer. "Murder." He offered no justification, only an explanation I found poignant— and tragic for everyone involved. "I destroyed two families that night," the man told me. "His and mine." Thirty-two years and counting, my conversation partner has yet to make parole.

Last week, the United States Supreme Court heard arguments questioning the constitutionality of sentencing juveniles to life in prison without possibility of parole for non-homicidal crimes. The Eighth Amendment prohibits cruel and unusual punishment. Justice Breyer stated, "It's pretty unusual to have this" and, at least for thirteen-year-olds, "it is a cruel thing to do to remove from that individual his entire life," while Justice Alito opined "that some juvenile offenders deserve life without parole."[35]

During the late eighteenth century, the Universalism that accounts for half our denominational identity posited all souls shall grow into harmony with the divine. By the late nineteenth and early twentieth centuries, Universalism took up the question of redemption in this life, not the next one. If we affirm the "inherent worth and dignity of every person," does that mean we believe the thirteen-year-old convicted of sexual battery and sentenced to life in prison without parole continues to have

---

34 James Gilligan, *Violence: Our Deadly Epidemic and Its Causes*, pp. 9, 11

35 "Justices Consider the Role of Age in Life Sentences," Adam Liptak, *The New York Times*, November 10, 2009

worth and dignity throughout his life behind bars? Or does our affirmation require us to consider his dignity and worth more consciously than he considered his victim's? Whether he acted in concert with the two older accomplices, or at their urging, what would our recognition of his worth, his potentiality as a human being—as a possessor of that divine light the Quakers say burns within us all—entail? What is the appropriate response to a thirteen-year-old who goes terribly awry? Is it to consign him to a life, perhaps seven decades in prison?

Saturday morning I arrived at the prison early so I walked for twenty minutes down the road to greet the Black Angus cattle grazing on the grounds in front of the minimum security unit. The prison complex in Shirley sits on the site of an old Shaker village, on land that was once farmed. I watched a large flock of geese forage in a field that could easily yield crops to feed the incarcerated men who feed instead on a highly processed, fat-, sugar-, and salt-laden diet devoid of fresh produce or sound nutrition.

It seems so logical to transform the sterile grounds into gardens, to provide food and agricultural training. Why stop there? Why not teach men horticulture? Animal husbandry? Why not equip inmates with marketable and life-sustaining skills? Why not grow roses and lilies, beds of perennials so beautiful that even the lifers could joyfully anticipate spring? Why not affirm life by affording the dignity of growing one's own food, participating in the cycle of life instead of fostering a downward spiral of inertia and negativity?

Legislatures enacted laws to prevent the exploitation of prison labor. There's no dignity to a chain gang or twelve-hour days breaking rock, but there is dignity in the opportunity to be of use, to toil honestly, to coax beauty and nourishment from the soil.

In the fourth chapter of the book of Genesis, Cain, the first son of Eve, became "a tiller of the ground," while his younger brother

Abel tends the sheep.

> In the course of time Cain brought to the Lord an offering
> of the fruit of the ground and Abel for his part brought the
> firstlings of his flock. . . . And the Lord had regard for Abel
> and his offering, but for Cain and his offering he had no
> regard. So Cain was very angry, and his countenance fell.
> The Lord said to Cain, "Why are you angry and why has
> your countenance fallen? If you do well, will you not be
> accepted? And if you do not do well, sin is lurking at the
> door; its desire is for you but you must master it."
> Cain said to his brother Abel, "Let us go out to the field.
> And when they were in the field, Cain rose up against his
> brother Abel and killed him. Then the Lord said to Cain,
> "Where is your brother Abel?" He said, "I do not know; am
> I my brother's keeper?" And the Lord said, "What have you
> done? Listen, your brother's blood is crying out to me from
> the ground. And now you are cursed from the ground, which
> has opened its mouth to receive your brother's blood from
> your hand. When you till the ground it will no longer yield
> to you its strength; you will be a fugitive and a wanderer on
> the earth. Cain said to the Lord, "My punishment is greater
> than I can bear. Today you have driven me away from the
> soil, and I shall be hidden from your face; I shall be a fugitive
> and a wanderer on the earth, and anyone who meets me may
> kill me." Then the Lord said to him, "Not so! Whoever kills
> Cain will suffer a sevenfold vengeance." And the Lord put a
> mark on Cain, so that no one who came upon him would
> kill him. Then Cain went away from the presence of the
> Lord, and settled in the land of Nod, east of Eden. (Gen 4:3-
> 16 NRSV)

Biblical scholars have not reached agreement about why God
disregards Cain's offering. Some suggest the story demonstrates
the "historical opposition of shepherds and farmers."[36] As I reread
the narrative now, I think of the fallow ground the prison sits on.

---

36 *HarperCollins Study Bible*, p. 10

Does the maw of earth open to receive the blood spilled by so many hands that lie idle there?

I think of Cain, the prototypical murderer. Though first, he was simply the prototypical son. His brother has outshined him. His God has disregarded his offering, denied the value of his labor. Thus he commits a crime of passion, perhaps to avenge the hurt he feels at God's undeserved disfavor.

The story begins and ends as allegory. We who read the Bible critically understand intuitively what the metaphorical language implies: the text is not meant literally, but blooms as an invitation to glean wisdom and, more so, insight. Cain worries whoever he meets might slay him, yet the placement of the story befuddles: chapter four of Genesis follows three, when only Adam and Eve exist. So let us approach the narrative for what it reveals about our ongoing struggle to understand our murderous impulses *and* the power of neglect.

I am aware there are serial killers and sociopaths the Biblical writers had no knowledge of. Most of the people who commit murder fall outside those categories. They are people like Cain who act rashly, sometimes inexplicably, sometimes understandably.

Consider the character of Cain as an archetype, not just a prototype. Consider your own experience of being slighted, dismissed, ignored. In this tale, God does not acknowledge Cain's inherent dignity or worth. The Biblical scholar Claus Westermann writes, "Inequality enters where there should be equality. This is what the story is all about."

A story of murder introduces the concept of inequity. Life is unfair. God favors Abel. A parent favors one child's accomplishment over another's. Some are born into communities of deprivation, families of dysfunction, a dearth of resources. Some develop healthy coping mechanisms and some suffer trauma so severe dissociative behavior patterns shape their life. Some commence existence with a genetic predisposition to alcoholism. Others emerge from the birth canal addicted to crack. Life is unequal. We do not choose our siblings. We just have them. Like Cain, we have not reckoned fully with what that means. If we are our brother's and sister's keeper, what does that involve? Is the Fort Hood shooter our brother, in his brokenness and fury? Is the thirteen-year-old who is now thirty-four sitting in a prison without possibility of parole? What do we do with our errant brothers who may threaten, wound, or even kill us?

How do we keep them? Will we, like Yahweh of Genesis, curse the ground beneath their feet?

Our forebears who lived from the tenth through sixth centuries before the Common Era when the book of Genesis was compiled knew nothing of modern penitentiaries. Thus Cain set out to the land of Nod, or Wandering, east of paradisical Eden, a fugitive and a wanderer: isolated, alienated, not so unlike his contemporary convicted counterparts. What compels me about this part of the story is that Cain "went away from the presence of the Lord," but nowhere does the text indicate that God left Cain. According to the narrative, God decrees "Whoever kills Cain will suffer a sevenfold vengeance." As I struggle to discern what upholding my religious values entails, I take this passage to heart. It may be, as one scholar notes, "In antiquity, certain criminals were offered limited asylum when uncontrolled reprisals posed a greater social danger than the criminals themselves."[37] Perhaps the passage suggests vengeance is not ours to exact, and even if the very ground of our being yields no fruit, it holds us still. The earth weeps as it absorbs the blood we spill. It may turn barren but it does not disappear from beneath us nor does it cast us from our being. Cain sets off to wander, a fugitive, but the story does not end there.

Verse seventeen of chapter four finds Cain with a wife who bears him a son, Enoch. Enoch in turn fathers a son and builds a

---

37 *HarperCollins Study Bible*, p. 11

city. As chapter four concludes, Eve bears another son, Seth, and so life affirms its own inherent dignity and worth.

For so many generations we have trundled off to war. We train young men and women, and in some places like Uganda and the Congo, some of us conscript children into warfare, force them to kill their own parents, and those children, damaged beyond measure, remain among us, if not our children, our brothers and sisters in the human family.

A few weeks ago in sleepy Mont Vernon, New Hampshire, four teenage boys broke into a home and murdered a woman in her bed and then tried to kill her daughter. In the same month, a gaggle of teenagers gang-raped a fifteen-year-old girl for two and a half hours. Police reported at least twenty people witnessed the attack or knew it was occurring but did not notify authorities. If these adolescents are not *our* children they are the sons and daughters of a neighbor, of someone like us who never for a moment thought at his or her child's crowning, as that small head pushed its way into this life, that infant would become an attacker or languish in prison for decades on end.

In war there are no unwounded soldiers and in a nation of two million behind bars, no one escapes unscathed. The bitter irony and tragedy of violence are ours to reckon with. How shall we tend one another? What responsibility do we bear?

What Is Next?

After Tuesday's midterm elections, you may be wondering along with me, "What's next?" How does a deeply divided electorate proceed? Will Democrats and Republicans, Tea Partiers and Independents find common ground or retreat to separate trenches? Already, we have heard a battle cry to fight, but I wonder, in a rived nation, is fighting the next step? I understand the impulse to stand firm in one's convictions. Our Unitarian forebears Michael Servetus and Francis David were martyred for the certainty with which they clung to their belief in the errors of the trinity. But even they did not seek battle; they sought freedom of choice. They refused to subscribe to beliefs incongruent with their reading of scripture, and they spoke out, but they did not assail others for disagreeing with them.

This is challenging territory: the not assailing part. It has been dogging me this week, even before the outcome of Tuesday's election. My sister called me Monday night. She is perhaps my greatest teacher; her lessons often come in the guise of my utter frustration. My sister moves through the world emotionally bare; and I am uncomfortable in the presence of her nakedness. Often, she calls to tell me someone angered her. She laces her narration with judgment I react to, most ungraciously I might add. My sister is autistic and part of her challenge is that she lacks the skills or the superego, in Freud-speak, to rein in her uncensored id, her rash responses. She sees the world in gradations of threat so there is little room to consider things. An assault on her senses or sensibilities is just that: an assault. Anger mobilizes her energy; as she steps deeper into it, she steps further away from the fear that dogs her.

That my sister is unable to engage in mindfulness because her mind truly doesn't allow her to imagine what another mind might be experiencing, sets me boiling faster than water in an electric kettle.

I get screechy and preachy in the worst sort of way with my sister, though I never mean to. I try to corral myself and find an approach she will understand, but in my attempt to get her to understand me I totally overlook the fact that she can't: that her world is so riddled with anxiety and a lack of emotional strategies many adults have. When fear is the only traveling companion, life quickly turns into an arsenal.

What scares me about the recent election isn't the results as much as the fear that fueled campaigns so often ugly in their tenor. When fake pundit Stephen Colbert rallied to keep fear alive alongside Jon Stewart's efforts to restore sanity, the pair contrived an easy ending where reasonableness triumphs. Sure, Jon Stewart acknowledged, there will always be the jerk speeding in the breakdown lane trying to pass everyone else, but mostly we drive in an orderly fashion, yielding as necessary so we can all get home.

I want to function within that vision and most days I do. But then, not so unlike my sister, something assails my sensibilities, more often than my senses, and suddenly, the image of my sister as a nakedly fearful person turns from portrait into mirror.

Take for instance the murder trial going on this week in New Hampshire with its grisly testimony of four youths charged with slaughtering a woman in her own bed and maiming her eleven-year-old daughter. I, the staunchest opponent of capital punishment, the one who volunteers in prisons to spend quality time with men doing fifteen to life, am so overcome by horror and disgust that I find myself thinking, there is no death painful enough for the perpetrators. The naked truth is, a decade and a half before a couple of young men wielded a machete in Mont Vernon, New Hampshire, hundreds of thousands of Rwandans died by machete. It's when the blade glints in a sleepy town not so far from my own that my fear roils; my inclinations toward nonviolence and my faith in the possibility of transformation evaporate.

For any of us, feeling threatened activates fear that unleashes anger—and for a moment the anger distracts us from the fear. Righteous anger distracts best of all, but like the vinegar-activated volcanoes of elementary school, once the fuming fizzles, what's left but a clump of wet baking soda?

What's next for a nation rife with internecine distrust and contempt? What's next for a divided Congress and a chastened president? For an electorate split between the disengaged and the enraged? What's next for a nation that often appears to forsake tools for weapons? A country truly targeted by extremists who find themselves thinking, for longer than a minute, there is no death painful enough for the perpetrators of what threatens them?

That's the sticky part: daring to even look for the *us* in *them*. I am the first to admit how much I resist that exercise. I don't even like doing it with my sister. I prefer to sizzle and snap every time she recounts what a pain someone at her church is, or how the pastor should kick out the homeless guy who sat next to her and suggested they ought to kill President Obama. I prefer to take deep breaths and explain how it is incumbent upon the pastor to follow the teachings of Jesus: to do for the least among them—the homeless, the deranged, the disregarded. Reluctantly, I might get around to admitting, not so unlike Juan Williams, that I would get nervous around an unkempt, possibly paranoid man advocating murder. I might give my sister that nanosecond of identification: I too, can relate to being afraid, though I know nothing of the depth of her fear, the relentless all-consuming anxiety: the only partner she has.

And then, I inevitably hang up the phone and despise myself for doing what I can't tolerate in her: I want so desperately for her to have more skill at clothing her responses. I want a world where all of us engage mindfully, where each of us pauses to consider how the other might be feeling, how another's experience shapes not only a world view but a way of being.

We may not agree with or condone the actions of another; we might not even be capable of imagining the means, but we do ourselves no favor if we don't try at least to understand the ends. Yes, psychopathology exists and it may elude all but the forensic psychiatrists, but teenagers who take up machetes and strap on suicide vests and assemble IEDs roam among us and come from wombs not so unlike the ones from which we and our children emerge. Anger cloaked as violence may be the only mask for otherwise naked fear.

When the adults start screaming epithets, when the politicians accuse each other with more gusto than gunslingers in the Wild West, when fear mobilizes anger to the point that ordinary citizens conflate a Nobel peace laureate with Adolf Hitler, confuse a constitutional law scholar with a monkey, decry a secret Muslim in the White House; when we who value religious freedom sit back and let the media skewer a female candidate for being a witch, what's next?

Some of the threats we face are real and my sister teaches me that all of the threats we *feel* feel real. If feeling threatened can make a peacenik like me reach—even for a moment—toward a violent answer, if reasonable fear can cause reasonable people to assail others who seem unreasonable to us, what can God or the earth or the thrum of existence count on us to do?

To be responsive, to read the news and try to comprehend the despair that descends yet again this week upon Haiti. To notice the ones in our neighborhood whose longing threatens to disrupt our own, and recognize them as neighbors even if we don't invite them to the block party. To understand that being responsive to others means we have a responsibility to ourselves not to get overwhelmed, and if we do, not to stay there.

We can acknowledge the relationships that bless us, the good fortune that underpins our existence, and know when to shut off the news and stand in the presence of beauty. Lie down at the roots of a great white pine or copper beech. Rest for a while under broad canopies that outlive recessions and even wars, gerrymandering and pandering, twenty-four hour news cycles chattering and blatting. We can unplug ourselves long enough to stroll in the wake of kindness, plunk ourselves down in the vast fields of compassion that blanket the earth as much as the schisms and horrors that defile it.

Because we are all human any strong emotion will evoke our own. The nakedness of my sister's responses threatens to undress me. When I hear rhetoric devoid of reason and chock full of fear, my frustration ignites far quicker than my compassion. And in the shortness of my wick, I catch a glimmer of my sister, who smiles at me in the mirror and says, "You *have* a choice. You can imagine what others may be thinking or feeling. You can perceive thoughts different than your own."

For all the uncertainty that plagues us and gives our life meaning, there can be constancy in what's next if we exercise the freedom of choice our forebears died for—if we speak up and cry out without assailing others. We can predict but not know, and in that uncertainty we can choose to fret or fume, to turn away in haste or slow ourselves with mindfulness. It's the consistency of our choices that can anchor us.

My sister tells me she will keep her judgments to herself. In her nakedness that is her fig leaf of compassion.

We dwell in the garden: afraid of its serpents, in praise of its fruits—together.

The sight of my sister's fig leaf makes me reach for my own.

Rising Again

Each year as I seek to find meaning in the Easter narrative I am humbled by the task. I come to it a Jewish Unitarian Universalist, deeply aware of the power of story. A story that has endured multiple permutations over two thousand years is a story worth revisiting. Whether one's reading is metaphorical or literal, open-ended or absolute, this is a story of brokenness and resurrection.

Brokenness carries its own connotations. Death, destruction, shattered pieces, cacophony, discord, a rift. We often juxtapose brokenness with wholeness, as if they reside in antipathy. As if what is broken must be mended. As if Jesus is fully restored to Mary Magdalene's embrace. As if the twin towers could be rebuilt, repopulated as if nothing ever happened.

I want to suggest this Easter morning the possibility that wholeness is neither antithesis nor antidote. Rather, it coexists: wholeness emerges out of brokenness at the same time it contains it.

Kate Braestrup tells her readers at the moment she learns her first husband has just been killed, "I realized that though . . . my beloved, was lost to me, I was still in love . . . and I knew I would love and seek only to love with the whole of my broken heart forever."

What does it take *to love with the whole of one's broken heart forever?*

We live in a broken world riddled with broken systems. Just this week, the *New York Times* reported "at least thirty" Haitian survivors of the earthquake, traumatized and displaced, who "were waved onto planes by Marines in the chaotic aftermath are prisoners of the United States immigration system, locked up since their arrival in detention centers in Florida."[38] What could

---

38 www.nytimes.com/2010/04/01/us/01detain.html

be more shattering?

I think of the brokenness Jesus ministered within and to. I'm not speaking of the doctrine of Original Sin, but of the prosaic nature of humankind. Jesus lived in an economy in need of radical readjustment. He lived in a culture steeped in values and assumptions that constrained human life. His contemporaries practiced retribution far more than reconciliation. The conception of God the rabbis would have passed on to him reflected a deity keenly partisan, a God known for wideness of mercy but also depth of wrath. Jesus ministered in a milieu of tribe and class. Within religious and political contexts where boundaries were unmistakably clear, Jesus stirred the waters and etched new lines in the sand.

He dined with sinners and tax collectors. He fraternized and identified with all the wrong people. He taught that love entails more than fondness for friends and ardor for the most beloved. It involves doing for those considered the least and despised the most. He counseled forgiveness in lieu of judgment, self-examination before scrutiny of others.

In the absence of brokenness, how or why would he minister?

Mosaics transform static broken bits into movement, images, shapes that render beauty and new life. We don't often see our own lives as mosaics, as conversations between what is broken within us and among us, because it's not easy to get perspective; often we lack the necessary distance, the vantage point to see the whole picture: how "many colors are used to create one color from afar ... [how] the surface is irregular to increase the dance of light," how the mosaic includes the hungry gull *and* the sacrificial clam.

In each of us and within all our interactions exist infinite tesserae, the small pieces used to form a mosaic. If we think of our lives thus far, the broken promises and broken hearts, shattered illusions and expectations, the brokenness of systems and isms and economies that fracture and fragment our integrity of being,

the ways we splinter and secede from the fullness of community—
the words of Julian of Norwich are a balm. *In our falling and rising
again we are always kept in the same precious love.*

Last weekend, I co-facilitated an Alternatives to Violence
Project workshop at a nearby men's prison. We spent sixteen
hours sharing ideas about nonviolent conflict resolution, yet
several inmates insisted some situations require violence, a
position also articulated by President Obama in his acceptance
speech for a Nobel Peace Prize. One inmate facilitator opined that
a lot of the young kids coming through the system think prison
is a party. A time to hang with homeys and act tough. What they
need, he told us, is a dose of the old prison at Walpole, rife with
sexual predators, draconian policies, long stretches in solitary,
and the omnipresent threat of violence.

That would teach them prison is not a rite of passage, not
just another neighborhood at the end of the street. The only way
some people learn is by force: brute, institutional, or otherwise.
Other inmates agreed.

His comment prompted an unrealistic if Jesus-y thought.
What if instead of sentencing violent offenders to the harshest
conditions, we sentence them to love? To an environment so
disconcerting, so unfamiliar, so uncomfortable in its beauty
and nurture and radical acceptance that even the toughest thug
would, conceivably, eventually be gentled by it.

What would bullies and punks from the mean streets where
human life is disposable become if surrounded by 24/7 love? With
healthy food instead of over-processed, non-nutritive edibles? An
environment defined by sensory richness. Beauty. Warm hues,
soft textures, soothing sounds, fragrant smells. Instead of solitary
confinement, time spent in community affirming inherent worth
and dignity. Imagine the *agape* Paul wrote of in his letter to the
Corinthians—the patient, kind love that endures all things; or as
Kate Braestrup defines it, desiring wholeness for another as much
as for ourselves.

What would happen if we were to fill the space between the shards of brokenness with that love?

What's instructive for me in the Easter narrative is Jesus's depicted return to earth, to the same place where soldiers nailed him to a cross, where his disciples betrayed him, where his co-religionists derided him, where justice eluded him. Not unlike Dietrich Bonhoffer's return to Nazi Germany or the unnamed but no less heroic denizens of Rwanda, Sudan, the Democratic Republic of Congo, who return to the site of genocide to rebuild their nations. Jesus does not give up. He does not recede to safer plains. Like love, or *as love*, he endures. And though the language is figurative, the power of the story lies in what Stephen Colbert calls "truthiness."

There is truth to love resurrecting us. The love that remains with us as we fall and rise, again and again. The love we experience in the presence of death. The love that insists we leave our comfort zone.

The kind of love that does not turn its back on the men I met last weekend. The love that allows me to believe a man serving time for murder when he says, "I'm not the same man who committed my crime. I've changed."

When I think of my own brokenness, the psychic wounds, the early patterns that influence adult behavior, I need to believe I am capable of transformation, able to rise again from the places I have fallen, from the hurt I have caused. I need to recognize the way the light glints off uneven surfaces, how juxtaposing pieces sparks new energy.

A mosaic is a conversation between what is broken.

I consider having such a conversation with Jesus. My brokenness and his, the brokenness we minister from and within. The divide between the haves and have-nots.

I inform him the idea of redistributing wealth is meeting with intense resistance.

"In my world," he tells me, "we call it sharing. If somebody asks for your coat, give him your shirt as well. Whether you like him is irrelevant."

"What about the ones who say, 'I work to buy my stuff. Why should I give anything away?'"

He rolls his eyes. He's human, after all.

"Why should the earth give you flax and cotton? Why should the sheep yield her wool? Weaving comes from the ingenuity of ancestors. Everything we think we know, everything we claim to possess, everything we declare ours to use comes from the earth, which is not of our making—we belong to creation; it doesn't belong to us."

Suddenly I get it. To give away our coat and our shirt as well is a way of engaging in creation. Amidst the brokenness, Jesus ministers to connect us by breaking open the tight bud of our heart that we may bloom.

Think of how the earth literally breaks open, sundering homes, bodies, lives. Consider the mystified Haitians airlifted to incarceration.

Into this brokenness, Jesus is reputed to utter, not just to those in the lap of privilege and plenty, but to the distraught, the distressed, the ones behind bars: "Love your enemies, do good to those who hate you, bless those who curse you, pray for those who abuse you" (Luke 6:27-8) .In short, love, love, love.

In response to the men I met last weekend who paradoxically insist there are circumstances where only violence can quell itself, I still wonder if love can.

To reach for love in the presence of enmity assures not safety, only the affirmation that no matter how dire the circumstance, how dim the prospect, we can choose light. *The play of light is the first and last rule of mosaic.* [39] We can return to the places where death happens and still find love. "We can't have our dear dead ones back, not as they were, not as we loved them."

---

39 Terry Tempest Williams, *Finding Beauty in a Broken World*, p. 5

But we can collect the broken pieces. The bits of clamshell and rubble, the fragments of hurt and anger and loss, the splinters of inequity, the shards of violence, the unfathomability of love. We can listen to the conversation of brokenness and hear in it what makes us whole. And we can love.

This Easter morning may we see in our lives mosaics of resurrection.

The Missing Years

On Boxing Day, instead of a regular worship service we had an intimate little sing-a-long. I brought my trusty banjo. My friends, Sarah and Jane, joined me with their mandolins, and a gentleman in the congregation played fiddle. We sang Christmas carols, which is the only reason I can think of after the service a congregant asked me if I'd ever heard John Prine's song, "Jesus: The Missing Years." I hadn't, so I went home and listened to the picaresque ballad; and though I didn't rush to download it, something stuck about the missing years.

The years from twelve until thirty are unaccounted for in Jesus's life. Of course even the accounts of Jesus in the canonical gospels of the New Testament were written after his death. There are no eyewitness accounts, no first-person reports, and for many Christians, the miraculous story of Jesus's birth and resurrection are taken on faith. There's one school of thought that Jesus traveled to India where he waded in the spiritual waters of Buddhism and its predecessor, Hinduism. I like to think of Jesus wandering through India gaining enlightenment. John Prine imagines Jesus a bit more anachronistically, backpacking through Europe where he meets his Irish bride, who never made it into the canonical accounts.

What intrigues me about the missing years of Jesus is that something happened during that time that must have informed the three years of his ministry we read about—whether it be exposure to Buddhism or Hinduism or other religious perspectives, or something far more prosaic: the kind of experiences any of us could have traveling, being a stranger in a strange land, being welcomed or rejected. So often, it seems, the moments that get captured in a gospel, or for that matter, a photo album, in the home movies of old and the Facebook pages of today, rely on other unseen moments that inform the rest.

A couple of months ago, a congregant gave me a contemporary parable about a young man standing in the center of town proclaiming his magnificent heart. Suddenly an old man approaches and declares his worn, scarred heart more beautiful than that of the younger man. "Pffaw," the young man scoffs. "My heart is in perfect condition and yours is full of scars."

"Yes," the old man acknowledges. "Every scar represents a person I have loved. I've got some gouged-out places, some tears, rough edges, all of which remind me to stay open to love, to risk giving, to accept the gift of brokenhearted love in return."

Humbled, the young man offers a piece of his perfect heart to the elder, who accepts it and gives him a piece of his worn and torn heart in return.

Who would want to go through life with an untouched heart?

I like to think of Jesus in India, not so much sitting at the feet of a great teacher, but up and about on his own feet encountering teachers in all their guises, especially love and loss.

Thinking about Jesus and his missing years, the ones that must have informed the three years of his ministry we read about, got me thinking about mine. The great folklorist and writer Zora Neale Hurston wrote: there are years that ask questions and years that answer.

Years our direction in life seems unclear. Years that feel decisive.

Probably most of us have years we'd just as soon leave behind as revisit. I used to think, if my life were a movie, I would have to get up and get popcorn. There were so many points along the narrative trail that would have been too painful to watch. I would have had to get Milk Duds during adolescence and popcorn during early adulthood and then juju fruits for my thirties. If I could have tampered with the film reel, I probably would have creatively spliced. Whole years might have gone missing.

I have often thought of the missing years as the ones that pose questions, but the more thought I give it, the more the missing years answer.

I used to think a lot about my father's missing years, when he moved from Tennessee, where he'd lived his whole life, to Florida. I have no sense of his life there other than he followed a woman he dated who had two sons. I don't recall how long he lived there or whether he lived in an apartment or a house. What car he drove or what friends he had. I only know he moved again to Houston, where he remained until his death. I think of the Florida years as the ones he left the theatre of fatherhood for an extended trip for popcorn. Even though my father and I re-established contact after he moved to Texas, I never spoke with him about those missing years.

Decades later, after my father had died, I experienced my own collisions, stumbling due to lack of light, and that's when I came to recognize the years my father went missing from me as the years he was trying so desperately to find himself, to piece his own life back together. In the midst of my own middle-aged search for meaning and purpose, I awoke one day with such clarity: he had moved to find work after a huge professional setback. He had followed not love so much as someone who could anchor him in the midst of uncertainty, in a time of deep loss. I was able to recast those missing years when I rarely heard from my father as a time in his life when he traveled inward, perhaps to grieve the death of his only son, and the loss of marriage and vocation. It was good to see the movie from his point of view for a moment, not mine.

I think too of my maternal grandmother, whom I never met. She died four or five years before I was born. I knew only that she left her children and husband when my mother was eleven, that she was tall and distant, and suffered manic depression, and her absence from my mother's life shaped my experience as a daughter as much as my mother's experience as one. It wasn't until age thirty-eight when I finally read the one remaining journal my grandmother had written. My mother had burned all the others years before. That one slender volume often recorded in pencil in a one-year diary with multiple entries on the same date from year to year answered so many questions *years of my life* had posed.

For the first time I saw my mother laterally: woman to woman. Instead of gazing up at her from the view of an ornery, grief stricken thirteen-year-old angry at everything she'd done, I saw my mother as a peer, not much older than I at the time, so that it was my mother, not me, deep in a crevasse of grief and loss caused by divorce and the death of her son. Each time I sipped from the wellspring of that diary, I watched the story of my mother's life unfolding a generation before her birth, in that way our origins precede us, coming to form long before we do.

I cannot help but wonder had Jesus left a diary behind, what years, what moments, what exchanges would he have preserved for posterity? What scenes would he have chosen to document his life?

One non-canonical account of Jesus as a lad casts him as a juvenile superpower who hurls a boy from a balcony and then raises him from the dead. I remember being struck by the humanness of Jesus's prepubescent anger, the way he, like other children's would get so infuriated he might push a kid off a roof without contemplating or fully understanding the consequences of the act. Or maybe boy Jesus *knew* he could magically raise the dead and could thus indulge himself in such an otherwise deadly act. Like all accounts of Jesus, this one probably reveals more about the writer than his or her subject, in the same way we all view the film of our lives from the vantage point of where we sit, at least initially.

Jesus lived what most of us would consider an abbreviated life—dead at thirty-three. But somewhere in those eighteen missing years Jesus ripens into a sage. For his followers he fulfils the mantle of Messiah. His miracles prove his godliness. And to the ones who view him not as divine but exemplary in his moral bearings, his ability to turn familiar ways of being into new postures of compassion and selflessness may well grow out of his missing years.

Perhaps it is our own years gone missing, the years that would send us out for popcorn, that provide the lessons, the humility if we have the graciousness to accept it, and the time that allow us to change seats. To watch the movie from someone else's vantage point instead of our own.

If my father and I were to sit side by side in a darkened theatre watching a documentary of years entitled "Missing," what years of mine would he miss me? And what years of his would I reclaim?

What years of *yours* are missing? In your own life? In someone else's life that touches yours? And what years of yours now past offer you answers?

Imagine there has been a video camera running your entire life, mounted in the corner of the kitchen of every place you've lived. Out of the hundreds of thousands of hours, what two would you choose to encapsulate your life? What moments would be most representative? Emblematic? Revelatory?

What moments would lend the most clarity? What moments selectively juxtaposed would explain our actions, especially the ones that appear most capricious or mystifying?

And if we could go back through the archives to view the tape, now mercifully digitized, of our parents and their parents, what scenes *of theirs* would inform our own? What slice of tape from the cutting-room floor could we splice back in for that "aha" moment when everything suddenly becomes clear? When the years begin to answer?

If we could take that edited version of our lives and mail it to anyone alive or dead, parent, child, formerly beloved, currently estranged, who would we send the film to? Who do we wish could understand *our* missing years? Could see where we really went and why?

Perhaps the gaps in our lives tinted so darkly by emotion or ego as to become invisible, the patches long forgotten, return to us not in full color, but as pentimento, a trace of an earlier painting that appears on our life canvas—sharing an etymological root with repentance. The faint image of a lost year returning when we have the hindsight and the humility to recognize its value, to welcome it, to see in that prior image not what shames us but what explains us. Not what condemns the parent in his or her missing years, but what returns him or her to us because of what has now become visible.

I no longer feel I would have to escape to the snack bar for most of the movie. Sure, I might squirm in places, like I do during a lot of films, but I wouldn't have to leave.

If the missing years of Jesus can lead us to revisit the years missing in our own lives and in the lives of those who shape us, they are not lost. Nor are we.

The poet David Wagoner, in his poem, "Lost," instructs us:

> Stand still. The trees ahead and bushes beside you
> Are not lost. Wherever you are is called Here,
> And you must treat it as a powerful stranger,
> Must ask permission to know it and be known.
> The forest breathes. Listen. It answers,
> I have made this place around you,
> If you leave it you may come back again, saying Here.
> No two trees are the same to Raven.
> No two branches are the same to Wren.
> If what a tree or a bush does is lost on you,
> You are surely lost. Stand still. The forest knows
> Where you are. You must let it find you.

So too with the years we are hesitant to claim. For if we flee them, or turn our backs as if that part of the forest does not exist, we lose ourselves, not the years. And if we still ourselves long enough to listen, to observe the branch as the wren does, to change position so that we enhance our view, all the years of our being will be found.

Wandering in the Wilderness

I was sitting in the office of an Episcopal priest trained as a Jungian, whom I had sought out for spiritual direction and counsel, when I heard myself say, "I feel like one of my ancient forebears wandering in the wilderness. Perhaps I am supposed to be here, but it's hard."

I didn't spend forty years in the wilderness; I spent four. It wasn't a literal wilderness; in fact I was in a city of 330,000 in southwestern Ontario, the most urban place I'd lived. What made it *my* wilderness was a sense of wandering, being uprooted, feeling disconnected from any sense of home, homeland or even myself.

I moved in 2003, after a profoundly tumultuous year, in the effort to make the best of a difficult situation. Canada had always appealed to me as a sensible and progressive nation, so when the opportunity arose to serve a congregation there, I went.

The first shift I noticed was the flat landscape. None of the rolling hills I knew from Tennessee or the mountains and forests of New Hampshire. Because trees root me spiritually, their absence stirred an existential loneliness that began the way dampness enters the pores on a rainy day and ends up soaking a person from the inside.

Next I realized the absence of familiar cultural markers. While the public library celebrated Black History Month in February, there was no one around who shared the personal meaning contained in iconic images of Martin Luther King, Jr. My friend's father had performed his autopsy. My sister had been born under the curfew that befell Nashville the week he died.

And then there was a feeling of exile that intensified every time I visited New Hampshire and had to leave again. I pored over the local weekly shopper each time I spent a day or two with my mother, imagining that I might drop in on a midweek event instead of flying back to Ontario.

In that way, my experience diverged sharply from the legendary story of the forebears who escaped bondage in Egypt only to be led into a desert where they wandered for forty years. The ancient Israelites, contrary to what their name suggests, had not yet inhabited what was to become their homeland. They departed the familiarity of Egypt with its constraint of slavery, and like many of us who prefer the devil we know to the one we don't, cried out to return. As horrible as their experience in captivity must have been, there were long stretches when it felt preferable to the unknowable wilderness. For in the wilderness, conditions were harsh, resources scarce, and the landscape desolate.

It helped immensely to view myself in relation to a larger story of ancient people wandering in an unfamiliar land, not knowing why or what was to come.

Inherent in the narrative of wandering is a sense of disconnection, yet, paradoxically, when we place ourselves within it we feel less alone. When we become part of something larger, identifying with an ancient story, we are no longer free-floating nanospecks in an uncaring universe. We are players in an epic drama. Conceiving myself as a wanderer in the wilderness invited me to seek meaning in a trying time.

Understanding my life through a lens of archetypes and archetypal events—figurative births, deaths, and transitions— gave me a more nuanced view of the journey.

To look at our lives and recognize wilderness is to confront the ways we find ourselves, figuratively, in exile. I'm not speaking of the literal circumstances and life-threatening situations of political refugees and persons displaced by war who experience physical displacement. I am speaking of a spiritual condition where any of us might find ourselves removed from the capacity to access the comfortingly familiar, to feel as though we can climb into the lap of what holds us and be cradled for a while. I am speaking of a sense of spiritual disconnection that may originate in any number of human behaviors: addiction, for example, wherein the compulsion for a substance to provide relief, to offer escape from one's own self-alienation, only serves to deepen the alienation. We might end up wandering in the spiritual wilderness because grief has uprooted us like a tornado and dropped us into a desert of desolation or despair. We could find ourselves exiled from the source of what grounds us by dint of fear or depression, which limit our choices by obscuring them. Or we might find ourselves wandering after years of living un-attuned to what connects us to the thrum of being.

For some of us, it's all of the above.

What I came to discover, as did the ancient Israelites, is that the wilderness provides a container—not a warm fuzzy one but a container nonetheless—for a set of experiences that have the potential to inform the rest.

There's a scene in the story of the ancient Israelites, as told in the Book of Numbers, the name of which in Hebrew is *Bimidbar*, which means "in the wilderness," where the congregation, as it is called, is fed up. They cry out to God in their woe: "Why have you brought us up out of Egypt, to bring us to this wretched place? It is no place for grain, or figs, or vines, or pomegranates; and there is no water to drink" (20:5).

How many of us have been there—crying out, "Enough is enough," or in the case of deprivation, "Not enough is not enough"? I suspect most of us know the feeling of being asked to carry more than we can. We look around and instead of seeing the normal plentitude we glimpse only empty stores: no figs, no grain, no pomegranates. Not even water.

It's at this moment in our own internal wilderness we are invited to relate to the billion fellow human beings who actually don't have clean water to drink: to realize our interior landscape is an external reality for one out of six people on earth. It is hard to feel alone in that kind of company.

But because alienation makes it hard to *feel* the presence of others even when they are right beside us, we too, cry out.

In the Book of Numbers, God tells Moses and his brother Aaron to "assemble the congregation and command the rock to yield its water." What's instructive here is that neither God nor Moses, neither Aaron nor the rock *alone* yields water: the water springs as the result of combined stirrings.

If in the wilderness we can attune ourselves to the combined stirrings, if we can hear our voice as one among many, feel in our yearning the pull of each being who longs to survive, we can tap into a collective force that summons humility and evidences grace.

What befalls us and what is bestowed upon us arrives on a wind not of our own making, but how we receive it—whether we welcome it, deny it, or diminish it is ours to choose.

While beloved hymns portray grace as an unmerited gift that appears unbidden, the wilderness invites us to participate in that grace. To take note and avail ourselves. Shortly after my arrival to Canada, when already I had doubts about my decision to move there, a woman in the congregation shyly asked as she exited the building one Sunday if I made hospital visits. I answered *yes* and asked who might want a visit. "Me," she said. Within a matter of months, she was in a hospice unit of a large hospital, where I visited daily. "You have made my dying easier," she told me one afternoon.

'Twas then grace first appeared.

The seeming wrong turns I had taken suddenly led me to a threshold of undeniable purpose. To ease the process of premature death for the one dying is an honor beyond words. It comes through the simple act of being present. And I would not have been available to sit at Sue's bedside were it not for the turns I had taken.

Wandering in the wilderness summons our presence. Unsettling, unfamiliar terrain gives no free passes. It demands focus as it enlivens the nerve endings and awakens emotion.

The simple gifts of presence and attention become magnified.

My second year in Canada, the mother of one of the few close friends I made died. I recognized being there is what afforded me the opportunity to be a companion. To serve as a pall bearer. That's when I understood spiritual exile is not abandonment. This is important because we often confuse the two. The universe does not prevent sorrow; it holds us in it. When Cain sets off as a fugitive and a wanderer after slaying Abel, he turns his face from God, but nowhere in the text does God turn from him. The story needn't be real to be true and a truth of the tale is that the connection is not ours to break.

Though it has become cliché to say a burden shared is halved, being present to someone in grief provides not only purpose but perspective. It regenerates connection. Grief is an underground pool that links one loss to every other. There is value in not feeling unique. In one Buddhist teaching, a woman asks a sage how to relieve her unbearable grief. The sage instructs her to visit every house in the village until she finds the one untouched by sorrow. To wander in the wilderness is to visit every house in every village and realize none remains untouched.

In our pain we are not always relieved, but the wilderness teaches that we are accompanied, if not by the ones we expect, by the ones who also know the dimensions of loss and the scale of despair.

As wanderers we may view the plight as only our own, but the wilderness itself sees the big picture and issues a cautionary tale.

As the ancient Israelites bemoan their fate and struggle mightily, they enlist a vengeful genocidal God to exact wrath upon perceived adversaries in language so horrifying as to place contemporary examples of genocide in the larger context of an ongoing story.

From the thirty-first chapter of Numbers, "Now therefore kill every male among the little ones, and kill every woman who has known a man by sleeping with him. But all the young girls who have not known a man by sleeping with him, keep alive for yourselves" (17-19).

In this wilderness, the holiest of holies condones infanticide and child sexual slavery. If read literally one shudders to think how modern perpetrators could read it as instruction; but approached figuratively, the call for such brutal desecration bespeaks an alienation so deep as to threaten the divine within each of us. Spiritual wilderness can be so disorienting as to unmoor us completely from our connection with the breath of the universe. When we become unhinged from our connection with the entirety of existence, when we can't remember what allows us to feel it, when we forget, in Martin Luther King's words, that "we are tied in a single garment of destiny," we resort to tribalism, butchery, genocide.

The starkness of spiritual wilderness etches our humanity in sharp relief. In it we will find the gruesome geometry of terror and the unbroken line of connection, depending where we look and how we act. For John Newton, the sea captain who penned "Amazing Grace," the harsh angles of slavery led him to a point of reconnection with his own humanity and the divine.

In a much milder version of wandering, far from the high seas or ancient deserts, I have learned the usefulness of time in the wilderness; the way it tests us, not so that we earn favor or lose it, but so that we refasten ourselves to what matters, reconnect ourselves to what sustains us, and re-member ourselves to the universe that always holds us.

Some of us perish in that wilderness and some of us make it back.

In the office of the Jungian priest, I recounted a dream (because Jungians trade in dreams) in which I stare at a wall covered with vines of electrical cords, frantically searching for a loose plug and socket.

I interpreted the image as proof of my disconnection. "I don't know how to plug back in."

I don't recall the priest's exact words but they echoed Rumi, who in thirteenth-century Persia wrote,

> Listen for moan of dog for its master.
> That whining *is* the connection.
> There are love dogs no one has heard of.
> Give you life to be one of them.[40]

My last year in Canada, I got a dog I brought back with me. She is of course a love-dog sent into the wilderness to bring me home. Every day we walk together on the dead-end road where we live, or in the woods that surround our house. The walk is equal part exercise and prayer. Each step occasions gratitude—for coming home companioned by a dog I would not have were it not for my time in the wilderness, a roaming dog who reminds me daily we may wander but we are not lost.

---

40 *The Essential Rumi*, Translations by Coleman Barks

Stop the words now.
Open the window in the center of your chest and
let the spirit fly in and out.

Rumi

Afterword: Some Thoughts on Preaching

Fred Hutchings, a seminarian in my congregation, interviewed me for a course on preaching. He said he found my responses helpful so I offer them here, with a grateful acknowledgment to William Schulz, who posed the questions in his course syllabus.

Do you have a philosophy of preaching?

If I do, it is first to listen: to what is stirring in my own heart, to what is stirring in my congregation and in the world at the given moment. Writing a sermon or Sabbath meditation invites me to lean forward with attentiveness and simultaneously get out of the way. Dudley Rose, my wise mentor, taught me early on that any response—effusively praiseful or sharply critical—is never really about the preacher. Or as the late writer and professor of English Don Murray said, "All response is autobiographical." These Sabbath meditations are my response to the world, to my own spiritual questions, to the questions my congregants utter explicitly or tacitly pose. The process is conversational. When I get up to preach I have the talking stick, but it is my turn to hold it because the rest of the time beyond my fifteen minutes a week in the pulpit, I am listening.

For me, that requires white space, or what Fred heard as "wide space," which I find even more descriptive of that space and time I inhabit while walking my dog in the woods or marveling at the striations of purple in the bearded iris that delight me. I have been graced with the opportunity to deliberately construct and maintain a fairly simple quiet life that makes the listening easier.

Thus to the question of what resources I find most helpful in this writing, white/wide space tops the list, followed by the interactions I have daily: walking my dog in the woods, observing and conversing with people, reflecting on experience, and reading, of course—poetry, sermons, op-eds and articles in the *New York Times*, prayers and columns by Joan Chittister, and anything else I read that lodges in me.

When I feel stuck or worse, empty, I ask the universe to help me listen. It is always an opportunity to let go and trust that the universe will present material, and it does. So far, I have not met a Sunday sermon-less, but I store the counsel of Jack Spong that it is permissible and preferable to stand before a congregation and acknowledge that grief or illness or brokenhearteness got the better of me than to foist a poorly written or plagiarized homily on anyone.

One of the challenges of preaching in a Unitarian Universalist context is that there is neither a lectionary nor a single liturgical calendar to follow, so most if not all weeks, the subject of a sermon is up for grabs. If a season or holiday suggests a theme, I usually avail myself, but in the absence of any apparent topic, I often turn to what keeps me up at night, or what keeps playing in the radio station of my mind. Sabbath meditations prod me past the hole in a fence I peer through with a sharply limited view. Writing them invites me to find the gate that leads to the other side of a question where I can poke around and listen and come away with a more expansive understanding.

To the question of what makes a sermon good, there are many more experienced preachers who publish tips such as including stories, humor, and insightful exegesis made real through example. I rely heavily on metaphor and unifying images woven throughout. But the sermons that stir me are the ones where I can readily tell what's at stake—for the preacher and the listener (or reader). Far more critical than any literary prowess is the unmistakable clarity that the content *matters* for us both in a personal palpable way.

In my ministerial internship, my wise mentor Helen Cohen taught me to construct a worship service that would always make room for and offer solace to the person who slipped in late with a heart broken open by grief, bad news, or a separation. No matter whether the service honors Martin Luther King, Jr. or celebrates Easter or wrestles with atonement at Yom Kippur, there must be a space for the person laden with yesterday's diagnosis of cancer or the death of a friend the week before. If my sermon is topical, in the other elements of the service I choose pastoral words that cradle, or I ask the musician to select pieces of embrace.

One of the virtues of a receiving line is the moment it gives me with parishioners to hear what enlivens, inspires, and weighs on them. More than any other skill, writing for worship demands acute listening. Each time I preach, a congregation entrusts me with its time. None of us get that fifteen or so minutes back so it is the preacher's responsibility to be of use, to choose words with great care, and open the window so spirit can move in and out.

And as to the worst mistake I've made preaching, it was to try to preach what certain congregants wanted to hear. I girded my loins and assembled material to construct a sermon of intellectual heft that would make clear the value of religion to the scientifically inclined.

I did not craft a sermon so much as I "took the bait"—which turned worship into a contest that left me feeling wrung out and spiritually bereft as a fish with a barb embedded in my cheek, flopping in the bottom of a boat. Never again have I preached anything I did not give my heart to.

When I taught persuasive writing I distinguished between constructing an argument (amassing evidence in an attempt to prove the opponent wrong and oneself right) and persuading the reader by enlarging the view(s). Persuasive writing invites the reader or listener to reconsider, but it does so by first acknowledging that the writer understands and appreciates the reader's perspective and stake in the matter. I operate in a religious context where no one wants to be *told* what to think, or believe. I come from and choose to dwell in a tradition that questions and reconsiders: where *midrash* (learned commentary) informs and reforms the text. That's why Sabbath meditations are never the final word. They are one part of an ongoing conversation that hopefully helps open the window. Nothing more. *Dayenu.*

Acknowledgments

With deepest gratitude to all my teachers in all their guises; to Helen Cohen for never giving up; to Dudley Rose for teaching me ministry by offering it; to Paul Rasor, Jack Spong, and the late great Peter Gomes for caring wise tutelage; to Frank Clarkson, Cricket Potter, Mary Giles Edes, and Marta Flanagan for invaluable lessons in ministry and friendship; to Kimberly Cloutier Green, James Patton, Calvin Sanborn, Michael Johnson, Mark Hagen, and Elizabeth Davis for being my priests; to David Mark for many years as my rabbi; to my generous Monadnock colleagues for granting me honorary belonging among you and to my North Central Massachusetts colleagues for your support; to the conferees of LOAS 1 2010 for your shimmering light and glorious song; to the circle of friends outside ministry who summon me to the window daily; to Carol Drexler for guiding me to mosaic-making; to my mother for her candid critique of my writing and unwavering love; to my great teacher and sister, Sand; to my father and brother who did not live to hear me preach but whose light is evident in these meditations; to all the writers whose work informs and inspires me; to Grace Flesher for key assistance; Sarah Bauhan, Jane Eklund, Kirsty Anderson, and Henry James for making this such a handsome volume; to Robert Levine for the generous use of the beautiful cover image; to Tara Stuart and Helen Cohen for reading the early manuscript; and to all the folks who encouraged this collection. Most centrally, I offer boundless thanks to the good people of First Parish Church, Unitarian Universalist, of Fitchburg, Massachusetts, who give purpose to my preaching and joy to my days.

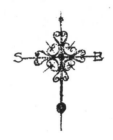

Bauhan Publishing LLC
7 Main Street, Peterborough
NH 03458 USA

Typset in Golden Cockerel by Kirsty Anderson
Cover Design by Henry James
Printed in Canada